Organisational interventions for work stress

A risk management approach

**Tom Cox, Amanda Griffiths,
Claire Barlowe, Ray Randall,
Louise Thomson and Eusebio Rial-Gonzalez**
Institute of Work, Health and Organisations
University of Nottingham Business School
Jubilee Campus
Nottingham
NG8 1BB

This report presents a risk management approach to the reduction of work stress, describing its origins, strategies, processes and procedures. It illustrates these through six organisational case studies. It is based on a programme of research and development conducted for the Health and Safety Executive by the Institute of Work, Health and Organisations, University of Nottingham Business School. These case studies cover 11 different occupational groups drawn from 19 risk management projects completed in collaboration with 10 major British companies.

The report is written for those competent in occupational health and safety and for informed policy makers, managers and trades unionists interested in that area. Some knowledge of the language and concepts of health and safety has been assumed, although its application to the challenge of work stress is explained. The case studies are deliberately presented in a brief and somewhat more 'journalistic' style to increase their accessibility.

Each of the collaborating companies received a technical report on their particular project(s), and the papers of scientific interest are being published through the relevant scientific and professional journals.

This report and the work it describes were funded by the Health and Safety Executive. Its contents, including any opinions and/or conclusions expressed, are those of the author alone and do not necessarily reflect HSE policy.

HSE BOOKS

FOREWORD

This Report presents a risk management approach to the reduction of work stress. It is an overview of the research and development work conducted for the Health and Safety Executive by the Institute of Work, Health and Organisations, University of Nottingham Business School (formerly the Centre for Organisational Health and Development, School of Psychology). It describes the origins and logical basis of such an approach, and the strategy that frames its processes and procedures. The approach is illustrated by six organisational case studies drawn from a series of 19 risk management projects on different occupational groups conducted in collaboration with 10 major British companies. The six organisational case studies cover 11 different occupational groups. Together they represent much of the private sector as described in the Labour Force Survey. The companies that took part were all 'large' organisations. An extension of the project to the special situation of small and medium sized organisations is currently being considered by the Institute.

Risk assessment is treated as the critical first step, one that informs subsequent risk reduction. Although the application of the risk management approach represents an organisational intervention in itself, there is particular concern for risk reduction at the organisational level. The emphasis throughout is on primary prevention; however, in all of the case studies reported, a balanced approach emerged including aspects of employee training, treatment and rehabilitation.

The Report is in three Parts. Part I presents, in seven sections with an associated bibliography, the risk management methodology, its origins, strategies, processes and procedures. Part II presents the six illustrative organisational case studies. Part III offers a statistical appendix and a glossary of key terms. The Report is written for those competent in occupational health and safety and for informed policy makers, managers and trades unionists interested in that area. Some knowledge of the language and concepts of health and safety has been assumed, although their application to the challenge of work stress is explained. The organisational case studies are deliberately presented in a brief and somewhat more 'journalistic' style to increase their accessibility.

Each of the collaborating companies received a Technical Report on their particular project(s), and the papers of scientific interest are being published through the relevant scientific and professional journals. Many papers have already been presented at conference.

The Institute believes that this project makes an important contribution to our ability constructively to manage the challenge of work stress, and hopes that this Report will be received with interest.

The opinions and conclusions expressed in the Report are those of the authors and do not necessarily reflect those of any other person or organisation. They do not necessarily reflect the policies of the Health & Safety Executive.

EXECUTIVE SUMMARY

This Report presents a risk management approach to the reduction of work stress. It is an overview of the research and development work conducted for the Health and Safety Executive by the Institute of Work, Health and Organisations, University of Nottingham Business School. It describes the origins and logical basis of such an approach, and the strategy that frames its processes and procedures. The approach is largely concerned with issues of work design and management, and their social and organisational contexts. It is illustrated by six case studies drawn from a series of 19 projects conducted in collaboration with 10 major British companies. Together these companies represent the private sector (of the 1990s) as described in the Labour Force Survey. The companies that took part were all 'large' organisations.

RESEARCH OBJECTIVES

The Report is based on what was essentially a research and development project to adapt a general model of risk management to the particular challenge of reducing work stress in large British private sector companies. It describes and illustrates a strategy and an associated set of processes and procedures. It does not represent a 'recipe book' or 'menu-driven tool-kit' for occupational safety and health practitioners or managers. The approach was designed to be adequate in terms of its application of science and to be consistent with current thinking and law in occupational safety and health.

THE REPORT

The Report is presented in three parts. The first part describes the risk management approach. It is structured in 7 Sections: these are briefly described below. Part II illustrates the approach through the six case studies. Part III provides a statistical appendix and a glossary of key terms as supplementary information.

PART I: THE RISK MANAGEMENT APPROACH

Section 1 provides the necessary background to the Report. It focuses on the challenge to occupational health and the healthiness of organisations presented by the experience of stress at work. It discusses its likely causes and develops the argument for managing work stress at source through a risk management approach.

Section 2 describes a general model of risk management as the basis for dealing with work stress. It describes some of the issues in adapting such a model for the particular challenge of work stress.

Sections 3 to 6 present the risk management approach as used in the series of case studies conducted by the Institute and as illustrated in the six selected for the Report. Each Section describes one step in the overall process, not only dealing with the practical aspects of its application but also discussing its origins and design.

Section 3 describes the first and critical step: risk assessment. It includes an overview of the method, and details the stages and activities involved in successfully completing an assessment. It includes a discussion of how the data collected might be analysed and interpreted. A risk assessment successfully completed should allow the identification of 'likely risk factors' for the health of employees and their organisations with a focus on the design and management of work and its social and organisational contexts.

While the results of a risk assessment for work stress are interesting in themselves, it is important that the information from such assessments is put to use. Section 4 provides a description of how the results of the risk assessment may be fed back and explored with an organisation. It describes the process of 'translation' during which any underlying organisational pathologies might be identified and explored in the development of a risk reduction programme. In all the case studies reported, this stage was found to be crucial. The feedback of the risk assessment data should inform the design of an intervention package to reduce risk. The emphasis in the current work was on organisational interventions and on primary prevention.

The design, implementation and management of interventions to reduce work stress are discussed in Section 5. This section largely deals with the decision-making processes and practical considerations. Specific details about the interventions used in the case studies can be found in Section 10.

Evaluating the success of a package of interventions is a crucial part of the risk management approach. Not only does this provide information about the effectiveness of particular interventions, but it also forms the basis for a cycle of continuous improvement with respect to work design and management. Section 6 of this Report presents a description of the evaluation process as used in the case studies. It also includes a discussion of the scientific and practical issues that surround the evaluation of organisational interventions. Many of the issues discussed in Section 6 are illustrated in the case studies in Section 10.

While carrying out the case studies, a number of important learning points emerged. These serve to highlight some of the main barriers to and facilitators of the risk management approach. An overview of these is provided in Section 7. More specific discussion of the relevant issues is provided in each case study (Section 10).

PART II: CASE STUDIES

Case studies were completed in collaboration with 10 major British companies in the private sector. Results from 6 companies (11 occupational groups in total) are reported in Section 10 after a brief introduction (Section 9). These case studies are offered to illustrate the risk management approach in practice.

PART III: APPENDICES

A full description and discussion of the statistical techniques using during the case studies is offered in Appendix I. Some sections of this Report contain terms that may require further explanation. To this end, a glossary of key terms is provided as Appendix II. This glossary provides brief explanations and definitions of some of the less familiar concepts and terms associated with the risk management approach to work stress.

CONTENTS

INDEX OF FIGURES

(excludes case studies)

PART I

THE RISK MANAGEMENT APPROACH

SECTION 1: BACKGROUND

The psychological and social aspects of work have been the subject of serious interest since the early 1950s (Johnson, 1996). Initially the focus of research was employees' adaptation to their work and work environments, and individual differences in that process of adaptation and coping (Gardell, 1982). However, by the 1960s the focus of interest had begun to change (Johnson and Hall, 1996) and to move away from how individual employees coped towards concern for the design and management of their work as one source of their problems. Common cause was established between work and organisational psychology, on the one hand, and occupational health, and health and safety management, on the other. This co-incidence of interest eventually gave rise to the new discipline of occupational health psychology. Not surprisingly, one of the main concerns of occupational health psychology is how the design and management of work, set in its social and organisational contexts, can affect the health of employees and the healthiness of their organisations (Griffiths, 1998).

A central concept in occupational health psychology is that of 'stress' and one of its main concerns is the effective management of work stress. The focus of this Report is the development and testing of a risk management approach to work stress, one consistent with current thinking and law in health and safety.

1.1 STRESS: THE HEALTH AND SAFETY FRAMEWORK

The basic health and safety equation of hazard - risk - harm has been offered as a conceptual framework (see Figure 1) for understanding the nature and management of work stress (Cox, 1993). A hazard is an event or situation or, here, an aspect of work that has the potential to cause harm. The concept of risk relates to the linkage between exposure to the hazards of work and the harm that that exposure may cause.

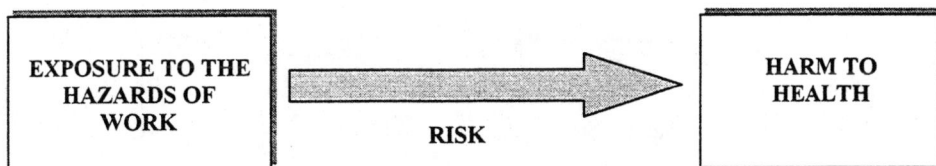

Figure 1: Hazard, risk and harm

The scientific evidence suggests that the experience of stress provides an important link between employees' exposure to the hazards of work and any subsequent and related ill effects on their health (harm) (Cox, 1993; Cox, Griffiths and Rial-Gonzalez, 2000). As such, it can be dealt with either organisationally at source, by reducing exposure to hazards that are experienced as stressful, or, at the individual level, by treating the experience of stress itself and its health effects. This Report is primarily concerned with the former strategy, although, as will become clear, most attempts to reduce the risk to health associated with exposure to stressful hazards necessarily involve both organisational and individually-focused interventions.

The analysis of the stressful hazards of work should involve consideration of all aspects of its design and management, and of its social and organisational contexts: not only the more tangible and physical but also the more psychosocial. Furthermore, where effects on health occur, they may involve not only physical but also psychological and social health, and, in turn, affect the employees' availability for work, and the quantity and quality of their work when present. If key employees, or a significant number of employees, are so affected, it is not difficult to see how the healthiness of their organisation, and its performance, may also suffer. Figure 2 summarises this argument. The scientific evidence to support it has been presented elsewhere (Cox, 1993; Cox, Griffiths and Rial-Gonzalez, 2000).

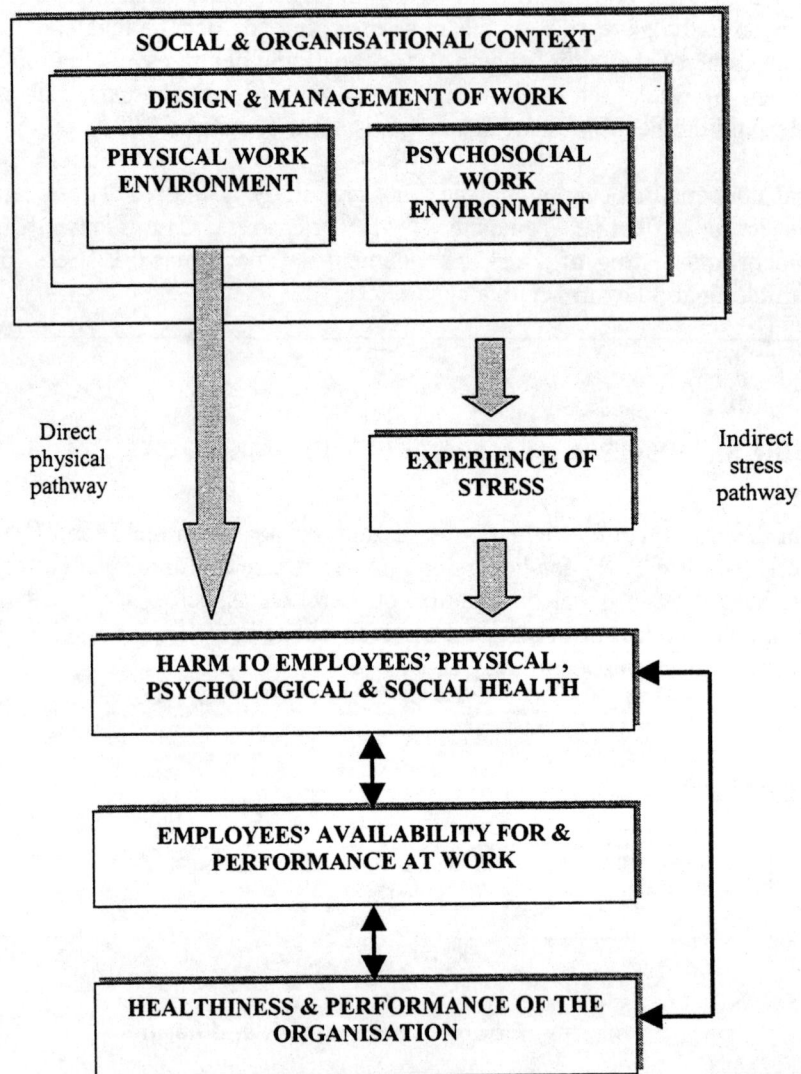

SOCIAL & ORGANISATIONAL CONTEXT

DESIGN & MANAGEMENT OF WORK

PHYSICAL WORK ENVIRONMENT	PSYCHOSOCIAL WORK ENVIRONMENT

Direct physical pathway

EXPERIENCE OF STRESS

Indirect stress pathway

HARM TO EMPLOYEES' PHYSICAL, PSYCHOLOGICAL & SOCIAL HEALTH

EMPLOYEES' AVAILABILITY FOR & PERFORMANCE AT WORK

HEALTHINESS & PERFORMANCE OF THE ORGANISATION

Figure 2: Work, stress and health

2

1.2 NATURE AND SOURCES OF STRESS AT WORK

Stress is an emotional experience that is complex, distressing and disruptive. Building on the model summarised in Figure 2, stress can be seen to arise from two different sources at work:

- Anxiety about exposure, or threat of exposure, to the more tangible and physical hazards of work.

- Exposure to problems in the psychosocial work environment and with their social and organisational settings. Such problems, essentially in the design and management of work, that have the potential for causing harm have been called "psychosocial and organisational hazards" (ILO, 1986; Cox and Griffiths, 1995a).

The experience of stress can be associated with, or can bring about, other changes in emotional state, in mental and physiological function, and in behaviour. These changes may often be benign and transient but, in some circumstances or for some employees, they may seriously challenge aspects of their health, their availability for and their performance at work.

> Psychosocial and organisational hazards were defined by Cox and Griffiths in 1995 as:
>
> "Those aspects of work design and the organisation and management of work, and their social and environmental contexts, which have the potential for causing psychological, social or physical harm".

For some time, there has been a reasonable consensus in the scientific literature on the general nature of the psychosocial and organisational hazards that employees may be exposed to at work. These hazards derive from both the content and the context of work and have been classified using ten broad categories (see Table 1).

Despite our depth of knowledge of psychosocial and organisational hazards, and of the more tangible aspects of work design and management, problems related to the experience of work stress still exist as major challenges to employee health (Jones *et al.*, 1996). The question is "why?". Hernberg (1994) has argued that:

> "the fact that classical occupational diseases still occur does not automatically mean that more research is needed. .... What it really means is that we have failed to implement already existing knowledge".

What has been long needed in relation to work stress has been a practical strategy for assessing and dealing with the health risk associated with the design and management of work, and its organisational context. At the outset it was obvious that such a strategy would have to be developed and tested through the design and evaluation of organisational interventions. This Report describes such a project conducted in collaboration with the private sector of British industry and funded by the Health & Safety Executive. About the same time as this project was being carried out, the National Institute for Occupational Safety and Health (NIOSH) in the United States made the organisation of work and related interventions one of the priority areas for its National Occupational Research Agenda (NORA) (NIOSH, 1997).

Table 1: Summary of psychosocial and organisational hazards
(Adapted from Cox & Griffiths, 1995, and Cox, 1993)

CATEGORY	HAZARDOUS CONDITIONS
CONTENT OF WORK	
Job content	*Lack of variety or short work cycles, fragmented or meaningless work, under use of skills, high uncertainty, continuous exposure to people through work.*
Workload / work pace	*Work overload or under load, machine pacing, high levels of time pressure, continually subject to deadlines.*
Work schedule	*Shift working, night shifts, inflexible work schedules, unpredictable hours, long or unsociable hours.*
Control	*Low participation in decision making, lack of control over workload, pacing, shift working, etc. Lack of control, particularly in the form of lack of participation, is also a context and wider organisational issue.*
Environment and Equipment	*Inadequate equipment availability, suitability or maintenance; poor environmental conditions such as lack of space, poor lighting, excessive noise.*
SOCIAL & ORGANISATIONAL CONTEXT TO WORK	
Organisational culture and function	*Poor communication, low levels of support for problem solving and personal development, lack of definition of or agreement on organisational objectives.*
Interpersonal relationships at work	*Social or physical isolation, poor relationships with superiors, interpersonal conflict, lack of social support.*
Role in organisation	*Role ambiguity, role conflict, and responsibility for people.*
Career development	*Career stagnation and uncertainty, under promotion or over promotion, poor pay, job insecurity, low social value to work.*
Home-work interface	*Conflicting demands of work and home, low support at home, dual career problems.*

1.3 HEALTH & SAFETY LEGISLATION: THE WAY FORWARD

Over the last 10 years, and consistent with developments in research, both the statement and interpretation of EU and UK health and safety legislation have broadened. They now cover not only risks associated with the more tangible and physical aspects of work but also those associated with the design and management of work, and its organisational context. At the same time, a somewhat narrow concern for the effects of work on physical safety and health has been replaced with a wider concern for effects on all aspects of health, psychological and social as well as physical. Furthermore, both the European Commission's Framework Directive on the *Introduction of Measures to Encourage Improvements in the Safety and Health of Workers at Work* 1989, and the *Management of Health & Safety at Work Regulations* 1999 (which represent Great Britain's transposition of that Directive) make clear that employers have a legal duty to:

> "make a suitable and sufficient assessment of (a) the risks to the health and safety of his employees to which they are exposed whilst they are at work" (*Regulation* 3(1)) in order to go about "deciding which preventative and protective measures to take" (*Regulation* 4, *Guidance* 30).

Explicit reference is made to the design and management of work, and the organisational context to work, in the European Commission's Directive on the *Introduction of Measures to Encourage Improvements in the Safety & Health of Workers at Work* 1989. This 'Framework Directive' states that employers should develop:

> "a coherent overall prevention policy which covers *technology, organisation of work, working conditions, social relationships and the influence of factors related to the working environment*" (*Article* 6:2).

The objective has always been to prevent personal injury through work. Earlier, the *Health & Safety at Work Etc. Act* 1974 defined "personal injury" as including:

> "any disease and any impairment of a person's physical or *mental condition*".

It is important to note that EU and UK legislation emphasises the need for employers to assess *all* risks to employees' safety and health, and then to take preventative action where indicated and to an extent that it is judged reasonably practicable. Such action should focus first on the employing organisation as the generator of the risk. The priorities in law are therefore assessment and prevention, and reasonably practicable actions (as specifically defined in British law) focused on the organisation rather than the individual (see Figure 3). The EU and UK legislation advocates risk management as the favoured strategy for taking the measures necessary to ensure the safety and health of employees (EC, 1996). It should be noted that, irrespective of any group-based risk assessment and subsequent actions, employers maintain a duty of care to the individual employee.

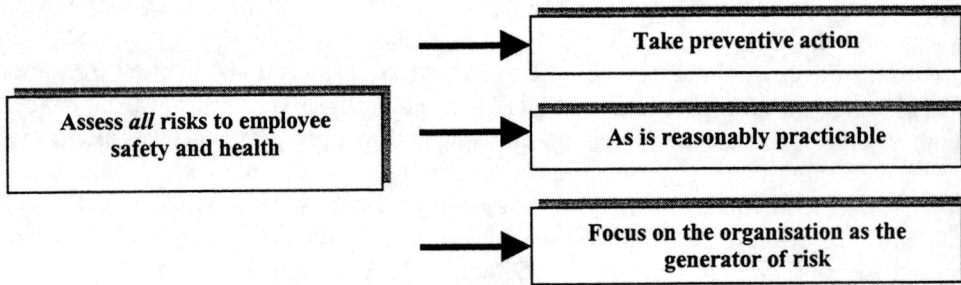

Figure 3: European priorities in managing health and safety problems

In 1993, Cox suggested that the risk management approach could be applied not only to the more tangible and physical risks of work, but could also be adapted to deal with issues of work design and management, psychosocial and organisational hazards and work stress. This is the focus of this Report.

1.4 THIS REPORT

In summary, this Report concerns the development and testing of a risk management approach to work stress framed by current thinking in health and safety management, and by the EU and UK legislation on health and safety at work. It is presented in seven main sections (Part I) covering the background to the project, an overview of risk management, and then risk assessment, the translation process, risk reduction, evaluation and learning points. It is illustrated through six case studies based on the approach in practice. These are presented in Part II of the Report (Sections 9 and 10). Part III includes two appendices: a full description and discussion of the statistical techniques using during the case studies (Appendix I), and a glossary of the key terms used throughout the Report, providing brief explanations and definitions of some of the less familiar concepts and terms associated with the risk management approach to work stress (Appendix II).

The research and development work necessary for this Report has represented a major project line within what is now the Institute of Work, Health and Organisations (I-WHO), University of Nottingham Business School. It was funded by the Health & Safety Executive. Originally founded in stress theory (e.g., Cox, 1978, 1993), it was driven by 'evaluation by practice' and was necessarily shaped by the restrictions inherent in research with external organisations in field situations.

The Report is titled '*Organisational Interventions for Work Stress: A Risk Management Approach*'. The application of the risk management approach in its entirety is treated as the organisational intervention.

SECTION 2: RISK MANAGEMENT – AN OVERVIEW

This Report is concerned with the adaptation and validation of a risk management approach to work stress. Section 2 introduces 'risk management' as a general strategy for managing health and safety problems, and then outlines the model of risk management used to frame the work reported here.

It draws on the model of risk management as logical problem solving. However, it sets this process in the wider context of a general system for managing health and safety as described in the Health and Safety Executive's 1996 publication "*Successful Health & Safety Management*" (HS(G)65).

2.1 RISK MANAGEMENT

The risk management approach to dealing with health and safety problems is clearly advocated by the European legislation and is described in some detail in the supporting guidance. It is, for example, referred to in the *European Commission's Framework Directive* 1989, and in the *Management of Health and Safety at Work Regulations* 1999. It is described in the accompanying *Approved Code of Practice* (ACOP) and elaborated in the *EC Guidance on Risk Assessment at Work* (1996). It is implicit in the Health and Safety Executive's publication (1996) *Successful Health and Safety Management* (HS(G)65).

> Risk management represents systematic and logical problem-solving, and is often based on two distinct but intimately related cycles of activity: risk assessment and risk reduction. This is made clear in the EC Guidance on *Risk Assessment at Work* (1996: § 3.1). This Guidance states that risk management involves: "a systematic examination of all aspects of the work undertaken to consider what could cause injury or harm, whether the hazards could be eliminated, and if not what preventive or protective measures are, or should be, in place to control the risks".

Risk management is essentially organisational problem solving applied to the reduction or containment of risk. Here the emphasis is on risk reduction. Various models of risk assessment exist in the health and safety literature. Most are structured and operate through a prescribed and rational sequence of actions. Decision making is a critical feature of organisational problem solving in general, and of risk management in particular. Einhorn & Hogarth (1981) have argued that such decision making can be broadly considered in terms of four interacting sub-processes: information acquisition, evaluation, action and feedback. The presence of feedback in models of problem solving and risk management implies that these processes are cyclical in nature and should be treated as activities that are on-going. It is, in this sense, that risk management is sometimes described as a vehicle for continuous improvement in health and safety. More sophisticated models of decision making (and organisational problem solving) are available in the literature (see Koopman and Pool, 1990). A typical model of risk management as problem solving is described below:

> Seven steps for the management of the risks to health and safety:
>
> 1. Identification of hazards
> 2. Assessment of associated risks
> 3. Design of reasonably practicable control strategies (interventions)
> 4. Implementation of control strategies
> 5. Monitoring and evaluation of effectiveness of control strategies
> 6. Feedback and re-assessment of risk
> 7. Review of information needs, and training needs of employees

Steps 3 and 4 – the design and implementation of control strategies – has to be broadly interpreted in relation to the management of work stress. The objective of such strategies is to reduce the risk associated with exposure to stressful hazards and this might be achieved in a number of different ways; through primary prevention, timely management reaction, enhanced employee support, and treatment and rehabilitation (Cox, 1993; Cox, Griffiths and Rial-Gonzalez, 2000). Although it is argued here that the priority is prevention, in practice the control strategies adopted tend necessarily to be a mixture of these various approaches. It is at this stage in the overall process that there is an obvious interface between health and safety management, occupational health, and employee support and welfare.

2.2 HS(G)65: SUCCESSFUL HEALTH AND SAFETY MANAGEMENT

The Health and Safety Executive's publication, *Successful Health and Safety Management* (HS(G)65), can be used to provide the wider context for the model outlined above. It describes the key elements of a general system for the management of health and safety, and proposes a model that relates these different elements through a number of information and control links. The publication discusses each element in turn. What is important here is that this system incorporates risk management and, at the same time, provides its wider context in terms of issues of policy and related organisation. The system is presented in Figure 4.

At the heart of the HS(G)65 system is a sequence of four activities – auditing, planning and implementing, measuring performance, and reviewing performance – which together with their various information and control links effectively describe the risk management process within the problem solving framework. Each of these activities is identifiable in the system presented and discussed in this Report. HS(G)65 is therefore a useful adjunct to the present Report.

2.3 OTHER POSSIBLE RISK MANAGEMENT MODELS

Various staged models of risk management exist in the health and safety literature, for example, Skinner (1962), Cox & Tait (1991), and van der Heijden & Stern (1992). These models vary in the emphasis that they place on particular stages of the overall process, according to their intended application or context. For example, Skinner's (1962) model for microbiological hazards places an emphasis on risk assessment and describes five stages: hazard identification, risk characterisation, risk estimation, exposure and option evaluations. There are special considerations in deciding how a microbiological risk should be expressed (risk characterisation). There is also a question of *which* risk should be expressed. Even if individuals are exposed to a pathogen, they may not become infected; if they do become infected they may not become ill; if they do also become ill they may not die. The choice of end-point (exposure, infection, disease, or death) is also very important. There are somewhat similar decisions to be made about the measurement of exposure; Covello (1992) has argued that instead of using a mean statistic or single estimator of exposure, risk assessment should work with the worst and best cases. This a strategy that is being actively considered by the Institute in relation to the dissemination of web-based information on good practice in the management of work stress.

There are now several substantive texts that together discuss not only the general principles of risk management and particular models (for example, Stranks, 1996; Hurst, 1998;Cox and Tait, 1998) but also their scientific and socio-political contexts (for example, Bate, 1997). All the models reviewed as part of this project incorporated or otherwise recognised five important elements or principles: that risk assessment is a crucial first step, that it has to have a declared focus (on a defined work population, workplace, set of operations or particular type of equipment, etc.), that it logically informs subsequent actions, that in turn those actions have to be evaluated using a multiplicity of measures, and that the whole process has to be actively managed.

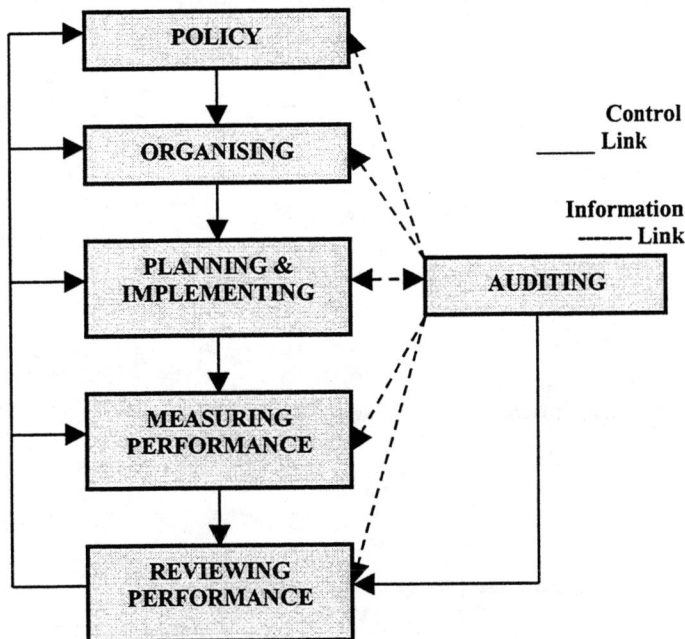

Figure 4: HS(G)65: a system for health and safety management

The general model chosen as the basis for the present research and development project is based on a general summary of systematic problem-solving processes as used both in applied psychology and in management science. Essentially the project is concerned with the adaptation of a general model of risk management to the particular problem and context of work stress.

9

2.4 THE ADAPTATION PROCESS

It is important to establish realistic expectations of what is achievable when adapting a general model of risk management for work stress. Two issues are important:

- First, there cannot be an exact point-by-point translation of models developed for more tangible and physical risks to situations involving work stress. There is a need to think logically and creatively when adapting such models. The issues that arise should be decided in the light of legal requirements and practical constraints, informed by scientific knowledge.

- Second, a risk management approach to work stress will not be 'rocket science' in terms of its specifications, the absolute accuracy and specificity of its measures or the mechanisms underpinning its decision making. Nor does it have to be. The goal is a "good enough" system to facilitate compliance with the health and safety legislation that provides a vehicle for progress in the improvement of working conditions.

2.5 RISK MANAGEMENT FOR WORK STRESS: FRAMEWORK MODEL

At the heart of most risk management models are two distinct but intimately related cycles of activity: risk assessment and risk reduction. These form the basic building blocks for the staged model adopted for this Report. However, in addition to risk assessment and risk management, other components are specified. These include 'evaluation' and 'organisational learning and training'. The model also introduces a new linking stage between risk assessment and risk reduction, that of 'the translation process'. Because all aspects of the risk management process should be evaluated, and not just the outcomes of the risk reduction stage, the 'evaluation' stage is treated as supra-ordinate to the other stages. This model of risk management is shown below (Figure 5), and is reflected in the structure of this Report (Sections 3 to 7). Each of the five components of risk management is discussed in turn. The risk reduction stage, in practice, tends to involve not only prevention but also actions more orientated towards individual health and welfare.

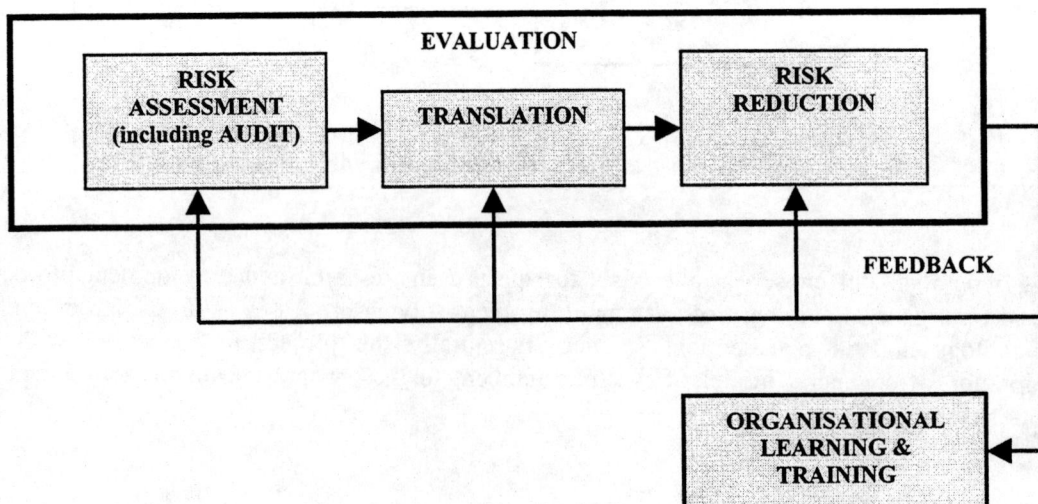

Figure 5: A framework model of risk management for work stress

There are parallels between the model adopted here (Figure 5) and the organisational intervention process being developed by applied researchers in the USA. The "interventions team" working as part of NORA (NIOSH, 1999) have developed a somewhat similar model based on an analysis-intervention cycle with an emphasis on the need for evaluation and for the feedback of evaluation data to inform earlier stages in the overall cycle (Goldenhar, Landsbergis & Sinclair, 1999) (see Figure 6 below).

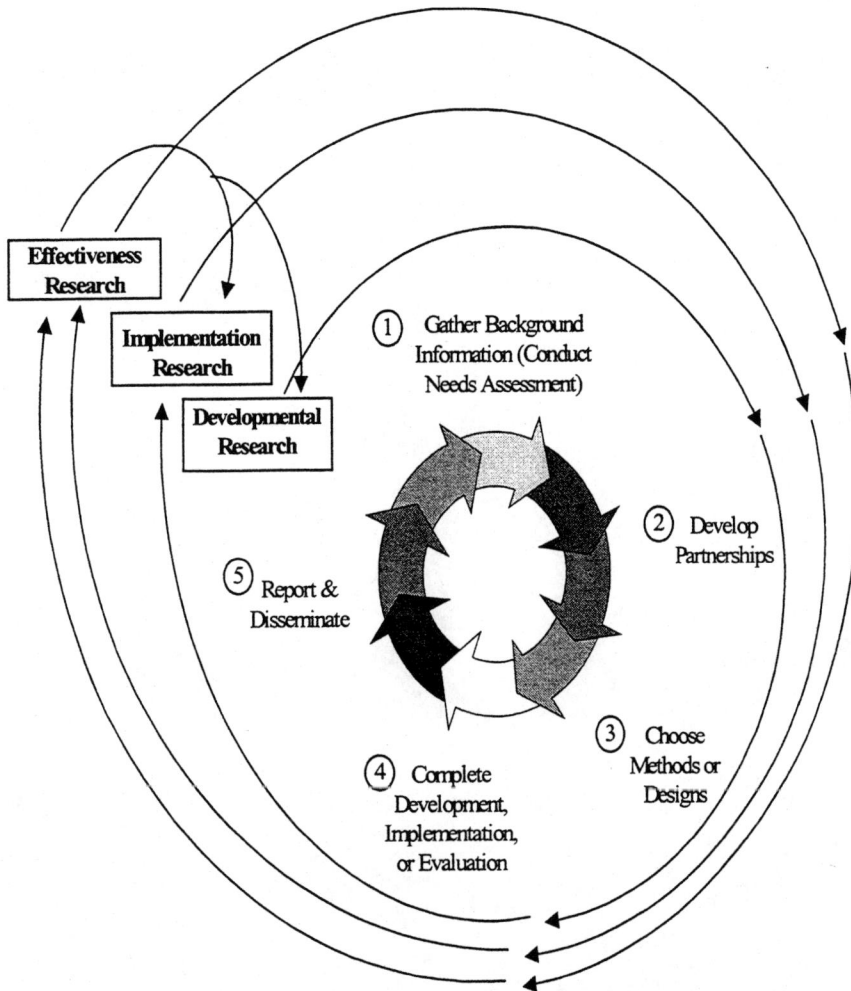

**Figure 6: Intervention research in occupational safety and health:
a conceptual model**

More recently, the Institute of Occupational Medicine, Scotland, has developed an 'Organisational Stress Health Audit (OHSA)', citing the work of the senior author and his colleagues at Nottingham, but focused on an analysis of the whole organisation largely using established research questionnaires (Lancaster, Pilkington and Graveling, 1999). Their point of reference for the OSHA as a risk management tool is the Control of Substances Hazardous to Health (COSHH) Regulations cited as 1988.

SECTION 3: RISK ASSESSMENT

Section 3 of this Report focuses on the development of an appropriate and adequate risk assessment for work stress. It is presented in five parts. The first is an overview that answers two basic questions. These are "what are we trying to achieve through a risk assessment for work stress?" and "given the plethora of scientific studies on work stress, do we need a new method of analysing stressful work situations and assessing the associated risks to health?". The second part unpacks the logic underpinning the design of the system, while the third part addresses the main issues associated with the design that was adopted, including the use of employees' expert knowledge and the related issue of reliability [2]. Part four presents the heart of the matter, describing in detail the various steps and stages involved in completing an assessment, and, finally, part five describes how the information and data collected might be analysed.

3.1 OVERVIEW

Two questions require immediate answers:

- What are we trying to achieve through a risk assessment for work stress?

- Given the plethora of scientific studies on work stress, do we need a new method of analysing stressful work situations and assessing the associated risks to health?

What are we trying to achieve through a risk assessment for work stress?

We are trying to identify, for a defined employee group, with some certainty and in some detail, any significant sources of stress relating to its work and working conditions, that can be shown to be associated with an impairment of the health of that group or of their organisation. This is the objective of a risk assessment for work stress.

Several points are important to note, and influence the design of the assessment procedure (see Box below).

---

[2] Some of the points made in parts two and three were presented in a keynote paper to the 50th Anniversary Meeting of the Finnish Institute of Occupational Health, Helsinki (Cox & Griffiths, 1995).

> **Key issues in the design of a risk assessment for work stress:**
>
> - Work with a defined employee group (see Section 3.3.2)
>
> - Identify significant (non trivial) sources of stress related to work and working conditions
>
> - Provide evidence of associated impairment to health
>
> - Use reliable methods to ensure the certainty with which conclusions about risks can be drawn
>
> - Work at a level of detail which can inform any subsequent risk reduction activities

Many of the issues that need to be addressed determine the quality of the evidence being collected. These reflect the nature of that evidence, its reliability, and the method by which it is collected. The likely risk factors that the current assessment will identify are at the level of the group, and consensus at this level is important both as a test of the reliability of the information and as 'part guarantor' that those risk factors are not trivial.

The assessment data should be used to stimulate and inform discussion within the organisation. This discussion will be about the need for, and nature of, any subsequent risk reduction activity. However, there are other, slightly more distant, but important, uses of the assessment data (see below). In reviewing these, it becomes clear that the economic arguments for organisations investing in risk assessment for work stress can be strong.

> **Risk assessment data should:**
>
> - Help promote the improvement of the design and management of working conditions towards better employee and organisational health and performance
>
> - Provide opportunities for organisational, management and employee development
>
> - Reduce the likelihood of claims against the organisation for breach of duty of care, and improve its defence against such claims
>
> - Strengthen the organisation's position with regard to employee liability insurance

Do we need a new method of analysing stressful work situations and assessing associated risks to health?

There are a daunting number of research papers on work stress and health covering almost every conceivable work setting and occupation, and numerous reviews of such papers (e.g., Cox, 1993; Cox, Griffiths and Rial-Gonzalez, 2000; Cartwright & Cooper, 1996; Borg, 1990; Hiebert & Farber, 1984; Kasl, 1990; Cooper & Marshall, 1976). However, it has been argued (Cox & Cox, 1992, 1996; Cox, 1993; Cox, Griffiths and Rial-Gonzalez, 2000) that the approach traditionally adopted in research into the nature and effects of work stress is neither appropriate nor adequate as an assessment of the associated risks. This important point may be eventually tested in law.

The traditional approach to stress research has a number of methodological weaknesses in relation to the requirements of an adequate risk assessment for work stress (see Cox & Griffiths, 1995a). Many studies have simply identified and listed stressors with no attempt to establish the association between them and related effects on health. While others have attempted to use measures of working conditions to predict particular health outcomes, their focus has often been on the particular health outcome, and the research has been conducted out of theoretical rather than practical interest. The measures used have often been derived from high-level theories and models developed for comparing different jobs. As such, they ignore aspects of work particular to any one job. The question has been more 'what problems do different work groups share?' than 'what are the problems of this particular work group?'.

Few studies have selected or defined their samples or populations adequately enough for risk assessment purposes, nor have they sufficiently allowed for the situation or general context of those groups in their study designs and procedures. Such studies appear relatively uninterested in the actual situation of the sample or population being examined.

Most of the statistical analyses used in such studies have handled data at the level of the individual employee and not at the level of the employee group (the assessment group). This reflects a bias towards dealing with work stress as an individual problem.

Furthermore, such studies do not usually provide data sufficient for immediate use in risk reduction. An almost unavoidable corollary of this is that most "stress management" interventions are often divorced from, rather than contingent on, the process of problem analysis. They have therefore to use off-the-shelf designs, and, out of necessity, target the individual rather than the organisation (Cox, 1993).

The answer to the question – do we need a new method of analysing stressful situations and assessing associated risks? – is 'YES'.

3.2 THE LOGIC AND STRATEGY

The logic underpinning this Report's risk assessment strategy was framed by current thinking in health and safety management and set within the general model of risk management described in Section 2. It can be described by a six-stage process:

[1] **Hazard identification**: reliably identify the stressors which exist in relation to work and working conditions, for specified groups of employees, and make an assessment of the degree of exposure. Since many of the problems that give rise to the experience of stress at work are chronic in nature, the proportion of employees reporting a particular aspect of work as stressful may be a "good enough" group exposure statistic.

[2] **Assessment of harm**: collect evidence that exposure to such stressors is associated with impaired health in the group being assessed or of the wider organisation. This validation exercise should consider the possible detrimental effects of work stress in relation to a wide range of health-related outcomes, including symptoms of general malaise and specific disorders, and of organisational and health-related behaviours such as smoking and drinking, and sickness absence.

[3] **Identification of likely risk factors**: explore the associations between exposure to stressors and measures of harm to identify likely risk factors at the group level, and to make some estimate of their size and/or significance.

[4] **Description of underlying mechanisms**: understand and describe the possible mechanisms by which exposure to the stressors is associated with damage to the health of the assessment group or to the organisation.

[5] **Audit existing management control and employee support systems**: identify and assess all existing management systems both in relation to the control of stressors and the experience of work stress, and in relation to the provision of support for employees experiencing problems.

[6] **Recommendations on residual risk**: taking existing management control and employee support systems into proper account, make recommendations on the residual risk associated with the likely risk factors related to work stress.

This six-stage scheme is represented diagrammatically in Figure 7 below. This figure provides a schematic summary of the risk assessment strategy.

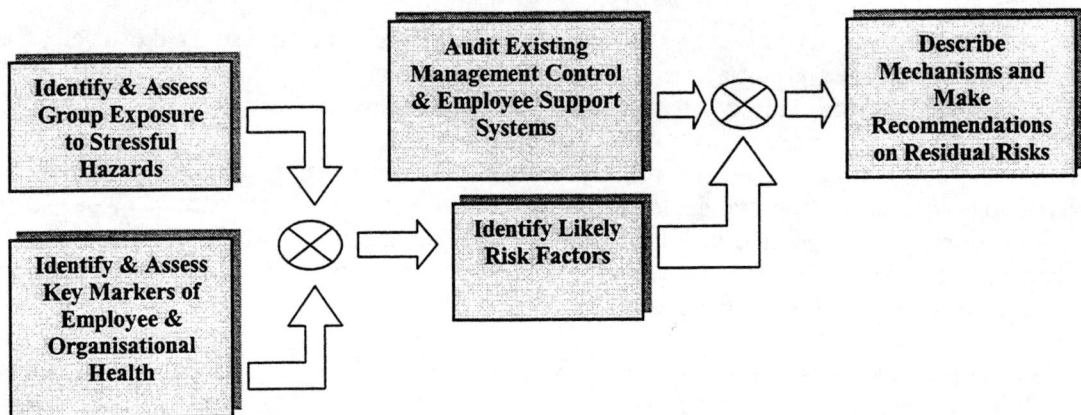

Figure 7: Assessment strategy

3.3 DESIGN ISSUES

The design of the procedures required by the six-stage risk assessment described above was guided by consideration of a number of scientific and legal issues: the key ones are discussed below. The elicitation and use of employees' expert knowledge, and the related issues of veracity and reliability, are of major importance.

3.3.1 The Focus on Working Conditions

The logic of the assessment method is partly determined by its focus. Existing UK and EU health and safety legislation is clear on this issue:

- The concern is for work and working conditions
- The focus is primarily on prevention
- The need is for organisational level interventions, *because*
- The organisation is the generator of the risk

Thus the risk assessment procedures were designed to provide information on the risks associated with the design and management of work and work environments, work groups and the organisation. It is concerned with the estimation of risk to health at the group level and *not* of risk to any specified individual. This focus also affects the choice of the statistical analyses used (see Section 3.6) and the subsequent design of interventions.

3.3.2 Working with Groups

The risk assessment method deals with work groups and the average worker as represented by the group mean. Therefore there is a need to define the work group being assessed, and a need to measure consensus within the group on the stressfulness, or otherwise, of their work and working conditions.

Definition of the Assessment Group

It is crucially important to define the work group being assessed, and this is usually done in terms of:

- The type of work being undertaken
- A specification of workplace or geographical locale
- A specification of organisational level

The group that is chosen for the risk assessment should be recognisable and meaningful within the context of the organisation. This is important for the assessment phase but is crucial for the design and management of any subsequent intervention. It is likely that the tighter the definition, and the more homogenous the group, the clearer the results of the risk assessment will be. The assessment group is also referred to in this Report as the assessment sample.

Consensus

In assessing group exposure to what are largely chronic stressors, some measure of agreement or consensus is necessary. Such measures will give information, relevant at the group level, not only on the reliability with which a stressor is being identified but also on the size of the problem.

3.3.3 Employees' Expert Knowledge of Work

The evidence is that the world of work *as experienced* is what drives individual employees' behaviour and, in part, is what determines their health (see Cox, 1993; Cox, Griffiths and Rial-Gonzalez, 2000). The hazardous nature of stressors and their effects on health are mediated by employees' experience and their knowledge of work (see Figure 2). That expert knowledge of work [3] must be harvested for a risk assessment for work stress through the use of appropriate knowledge elicitation techniques. However, there is, among many employers, a fundamental mistrust of asking working people about their work. The common assumptions are that such data are inherently unreliable and biased.

The assumptions of unreliability and bias grow from the belief that the 'employee' is *not* a scientist (cf. Kelly, 1955), is incapable of proper reflection, is unreasonable, self-seeking and politically motivated, and is naturally 'a deceiver'. These are unsubstantiated beliefs but are frequently offered in rejection of employee involvement in the risk assessment process. Their rejection is essentially a political position often adopted as a defence against the possibility of organisational change. What this argument does establish, however, is the need to check the reliability and veracity both of the techniques that are used to harvest employees' expert knowledge, and of the data collected. This can be done in a number of ways that may be used in combination to increase confidence in the assessment process.

In many situations, face validity (the common perception that the data are valid) is not a particularly powerful device. However, in the assessment situation, its importance cannot be under-estimated both as a test of the veracity (and acceptability) of the assessment data and as an initiation of the subsequent process of intervention. As such, establishing the face validity of the assessment data is an important part of the translation process (see Sections 4 & 5).

Establishing the reliability & veracity of employees' expert knowledge of stressors by:

- Auditing the design of the measurement scales used against good scientific (psychometric) practice
- Formally testing the reliability (internal and test-retest) of those scales
- Measuring consensus (agreement) within the assessment group
- Triangulating the self report data with other sources of information available in the organisation, to 'paint the big picture'
- Formally testing the concurrent validity of the data against health-related outcomes
- Testing the conceptual validity of the data against established findings in the scientific literature
- Testing the face validity of the data by feeding it back to the assessment group.

---

[3] Prevailing theories of expertise have been developed primarily in relation to intellectual tasks, but Scribner (1990) has argued convincingly that *all* work involves complex forms of practical and creative thinking. This view is echoed by Laufer and Glick (1998). Experience of work leads naturally to some degree of knowledge of it, or about it, and therefore to some expertise in relation to its problems and to problem solving.

3.3.4 Conceptualisation of Stressors

Deciding what are and what are not stressors is far from straightforward. It has often proved difficult in relation to the more tangible area of physical hazards[4], and there are many important questions to be answered in relation to psychosocial and organisational hazards. For example, should the definition of psychosocial and organisational hazards include aspects of work and organisations such as 'corporate policies, paid leaves of absence, promotion, health insurance coverage, etc.' (Landy *et al.*, 1994), even if the presence or absence of such things can be associated with harm to employee health? Furthermore, psychosocial and organisational hazards can often be conceptualised as part of a continuum that is represented by the hazard at one end and by the complementary health-enhancing factor at the other (for example, from *very low* to *very high* job control). Physical hazards, such as exposure to asbestos, often have a very different structure being negative per se without offering any obvious benefit for employee health. Other than not being present, they lack any potential health-enhancing role.

Further checks on the reliability & veracity of employees' expert knowledge of stressors:

- Social desirability effects (a common source of bias) can be tested for and screened out at several stages in the development of the assessment (Ferguson & Cox, 1994).

- Respondents' patterns of reporting can be examined for halo effects: any evidence of differential effects would reduce the likelihood of the assessment data being driven by halo or similar effects (for example, negative affectivity).

- The use of different measurement techniques and different sources of data should reduce the likelihood of common method variance (Jick, 1979).

3.3.5 Measurement of Harm and Health

The definition and measurement of harm is no less challenging than those of stressors. It is not a simple task to achieve a reliable classification of harms, or measures of degrees of harm, even when one is concerned with physical rather than psychological or social outcomes. Moreover, a number of studies (Landy *et al.*, 1994; Kasl, 1986, 1990; Johnson, 1996) have identified the difficulties encountered when researchers and practitioners have to decide on what particular indicators of harm they should use. Many such indicators, in practice, are flawed due to self-selection effects, complex methods of measurement and usage, recording and reporting problems, or confounding variables (uncontrollable, or unmeasured, influences on the data). A good example is offered here by the unreliable nature of medical certificates provided by general practitioners for absence from work.

---

[4] For example, there is currently an Internet-based project sponsored by the OECD to harmonise the definitions of the basic generic terms involved in the risk assessment of chemical hazards (OECD 1997)

3.3.6 Individual Differences

The estimation of risk at the group level is effectively the estimation of risk for the average employee, and can be contrasted with the estimation of risk for any specified individual. Where there is much difference between the two, then individual differences obviously exist. There are several points to note here. First, the individual differences that exist can only operate through the person's interaction with their work environment (etc.). There is no other logical pathway by which their effects can be made manifest. Second, there is no evidence that the individual differences that exist in respect to the effects of stressors on health, are any greater (or less) than those that exist in relation to other health hazards. Therefore, the existence of individual differences does not negate the overall assessment exercise. Rather, it adds an important extra dimension, and opens up questions about moderators (those factors that influence the strength and behaviour) of the stressor-health relationship. It should be noted here that despite these arguments and the fact of any group-based risk assessments, employers still have a duty of care to the individual.

3.3.7 'Rocket-Science'

Because of the state of current knowledge and because of the very nature of the problem, the quantification of the key variables in the assessment process and the estimation of risk cannot be 'rocket science'. Indeed, one has to guard carefully against false accuracy. One has also to guard against allowing an unrealistic quest for more precise quantification to distract from the management of the key process issues (see Sections 4 through 7).

Not being 'rocket science' is not a problem in that legally a risk assessment has to be 'suitable and sufficient' (Management of Health and Safety at Work Regulations, 1999 (Regulation 3(1)) rather than perfect, or the ideal. The assessment has to be good enough to identify major threats to worker health and does not have to be refined sufficiently to pick up all the different nuances of complaint that could exist in any work group. Decided cases and agreed out-of-court settlements (see, for example, Griffiths, Cox & Stokes, 1996) can be used to 'benchmark' this exercise. An assessment must be good enough to detect, at the very least, the sort of stress-related problems that have been the subject of successful cases and settlements such as Walker vs Northumberland County Council (Industrial Relations Law Reports 35, 1995).

3.4 THE ASSESSMENT METHOD

This part of the Report sets out the practical steps involved in making a risk assessment for work stress. It concerns the overall strategy and the process by which that strategy can be applied in any particular situation.

Throughout this method of risk assessment for work stress, three important things must be borne in mind and their implications fully understood.

The method is not an off-the-shelf recipe to be mechanically followed, nor is it a set of universally applicable measures.

What is offered is a methodology: a strategy and a supporting process. Adherence to the logic and the principles that underpin the strategy and process are the important features of this approach. This has to be so because of the uniqueness of the work situation of each group of employees assessed.

The assessment process as applied, and the data collected, will vary according to a number of factors – factors that vary from organisation to organisation, and between assessment groups within the same organisation. The process is context dependent.

While maintaining the overall strategy, the process must be tailored to the needs and the situation of each assessment group. This may involve little change or it may require thoughtful modification of what is done and how it is done. The data collected will relate specifically to the group assessed and its work situation. It should be sufficiently detailed to allow the design of any interventions necessary for that group. This is not to say that, at an appropriate level, aspects of the assessment process and of the data cannot be generalised to other groups within the organisation, or even across organisations. This issue is an empirical one and is dealt with later (see Section 6).

The assessment process does not specify particular measures that must be used.

In all organisations, there should already exist some form of data collection, assessment, monitoring or surveillance systems, and related organisational records. Furthermore, special projects using particular measurement devices may have been conducted. A risk assessment should work within the framework of what is available given that:

- The measures used can be defended as psychometrically sound, appropriate for the task in hand, and properly applied and interpreted

- The measures provide sufficient information for the successful completion of the whole risk assessment against its stated objectives

Depending on how good they are, and how well they contribute to the overall assessment, existing measures may need to be supplemented or developed. What is important is collecting information that together allows the logic of the risk assessment to be worked through, conclusions drawn and justified, and recommendations made and supported by evidence.

3.5 TAILORING THE RISK ASSESSMENT

The risk assessment method must be tailored to the needs and situation of the particular group being assessed and to those of the organisation.

The extent to which any one group of employees shares problems with any other group is an important question, and one that can only be answered empirically. Undoubtedly there will be problems that, at some level of analysis, will be common across different work groups, workplaces, organisations or sectors: there will be others that will not.

The fact that a problem is not shared by many different groups does not mean that it is not important. An assessment that is capable only of dealing with the high level problems that are common across many different work groups is unlikely to prove adequate or appropriate in law with respect to the needs of any particular assessment group. Some degree of tailoring of the overall method to the specific situation of a defined work group is both practically *and* legally necessary. However, the acceptance of the need to define assessment groups and tailor risk assessments to their situation does not mean that each assessment has to "re-invent the wheel" from first principles. The general principles underpinning the assessment method hold wherever and whenever they are applied.

The tailoring process operates in respect to:

- The management of the assessment process to reflect the nature and political realities of the assessment group and the organisation

- The design of the instrument for identifying and assessing exposure to work stressors to reflect the reality of the assessment group's needs and situation

- The choice of measures to include for health-related outcomes to ensure coverage of all likely forms of harm. This choice may also be guided by the need to benchmark against existing normative data

---

The objective of a risk assessment for work stress:

The risk assessment strategy and procedures used here were designed:

- For use with a defined and meaningful group of employees

- To identify, with some certainty and in some detail, non-trivial sources of stress relating to the work done by the group of employees and to their working conditions

- To identify sources of stress relating to the work done and the working conditions that are associated with an impairment of the health of the group or of the organisation

These sources of stress are termed *likely risk factors*.

3.6 THE OVERALL STRATEGY

The identification of likely risk factors associated with work stress begins with the exploration of employees' expert knowledge of their work and working conditions. Their judgements on the adequacy (or acceptability) of important aspects of their work are central to the assessment process. Consensus within the assessment group on these situational judgements on work is an indication not only of the reliability of such judgements but also of the group's exposure to work stressors. The reliability of employees' expert judgements can be established in a variety of ways (see earlier Section 3.3).

The possible relationship between the stressors as identified by the group and their effects on health is treated as the basis for identifying likely risk factors. In the majority of situations, this relationship will be one of association, rather than causal, and will be the subject of either logical argument or statistical proof. Where statistical techniques are available, it may be most appropriate to use Odds Ratios, giving a group-level association appropriate to an expert judgement on work characteristics (see Appendix I).

The likely risks are balanced against the results of an audit of existing management control and employee support systems. At this stage, consideration can also be given to the possible impact of the positive aspects of work on health. This 'balancing' allows some understanding of the residual risk to health. It is the notion of residual risk to health that provides the basis for the recommendations made and for the design of any subsequent interventions. A summary of this strategy was provided earlier in Figure 7.

In addition to the identification of likely risk factors and recommendations on residual risk, the assessment strategy and procedures allow for the identification of the major problems that might exist in relation to work and working conditions other than those affecting health (see Figure 8 below). These are the aspects of work and work conditions judged as inadequate by the majority of the assessment group, but not necessarily associated with any health outcomes. This provides a different sort of management information from that on likely risk factors.

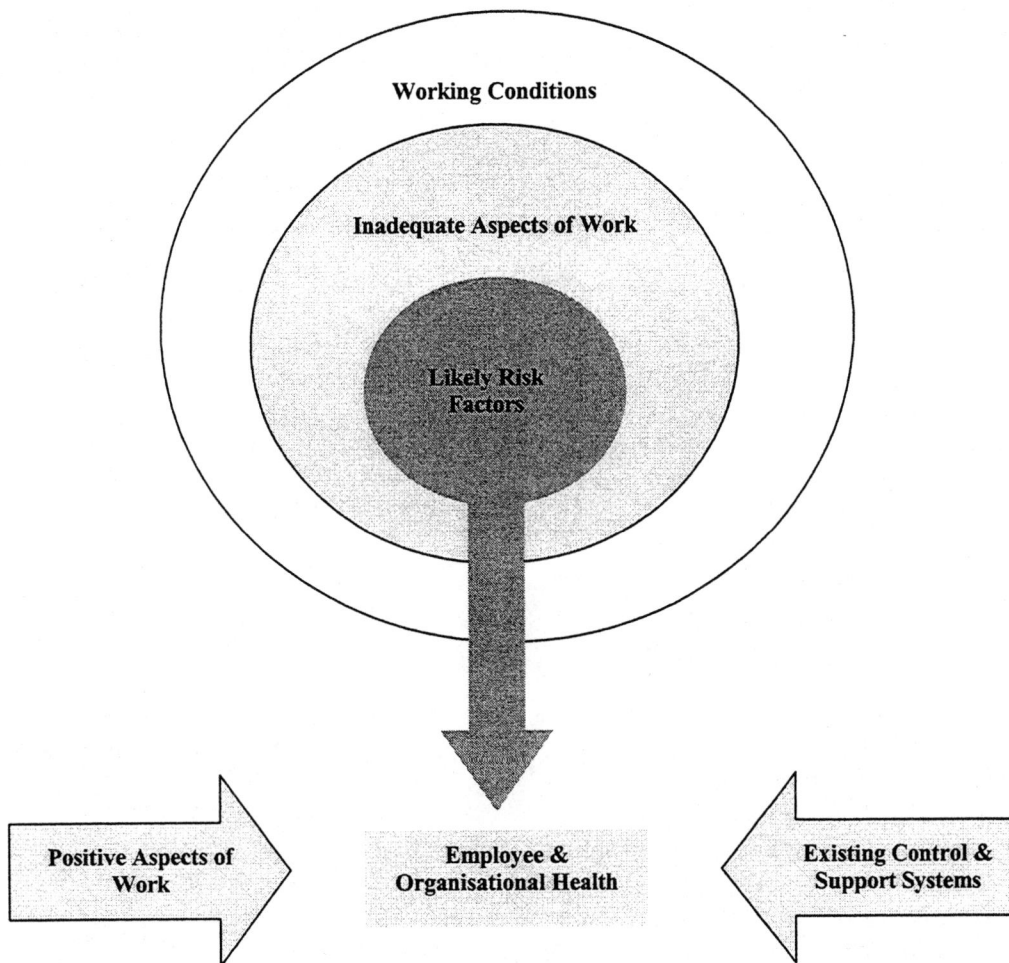

Figure 8: Working conditions, inadequate aspects of work and likely risk factors

3.7 FIVE STEPS TO A RISK ASSESSMENT FOR WORK STRESS

The assessment process in practice can be summarised in five steps. These are described below. The related process issues are discussed later in this section.

> **The five steps for the risk assessment for work stress:**
>
> - Step 1: Familiarisation
>
> - Step 2: Work Analysis Interviews
>
> - Step 3: Assessment Survey
>
> - Step 4: Audit of Existing Management Control and Employee Support Systems
>
> - Step 5: Analysis and Interpretation of Assessment Data

Each step builds on information collected during the preceding steps. The initial steps (Steps 1 and 2) were designed to build a model of the work and working conditions of the assessment group that was good enough to support the design and later use of the assessment instrument (Step 3). This instrument would quantify the group's exposure to all the significant stressors associated with its work and working conditions, and assess its health effects.

The five steps are largely sequential with one possible exception. The audit of existing management control and employee support systems can be conducted either:

- In parallel with the *Work Analysis Interviews* or

- Following the *Analysis and Interpretation of Assessment Data*

It is often most convenient to conduct it in parallel with the Work Analysis Interviews. In this case, the information collected can usefully contribute to the working model of the assessment group's situation.

The different steps involve a range of activities and call on different types of skill. In the work described in this Report, this challenge was met effectively through team work. In each case study reported here (and in all those reported elsewhere), the risk assessments (and subsequent interventions) were conducted by at least two people working closely together. These people were selected, as appropriate to the case study, from a larger group of applied researchers all of whom were competent in relation to risk assessments for work stress.

These five steps can be mapped onto the overall assessment strategy (see Figure 7 above) as shown in Figure 9 below.

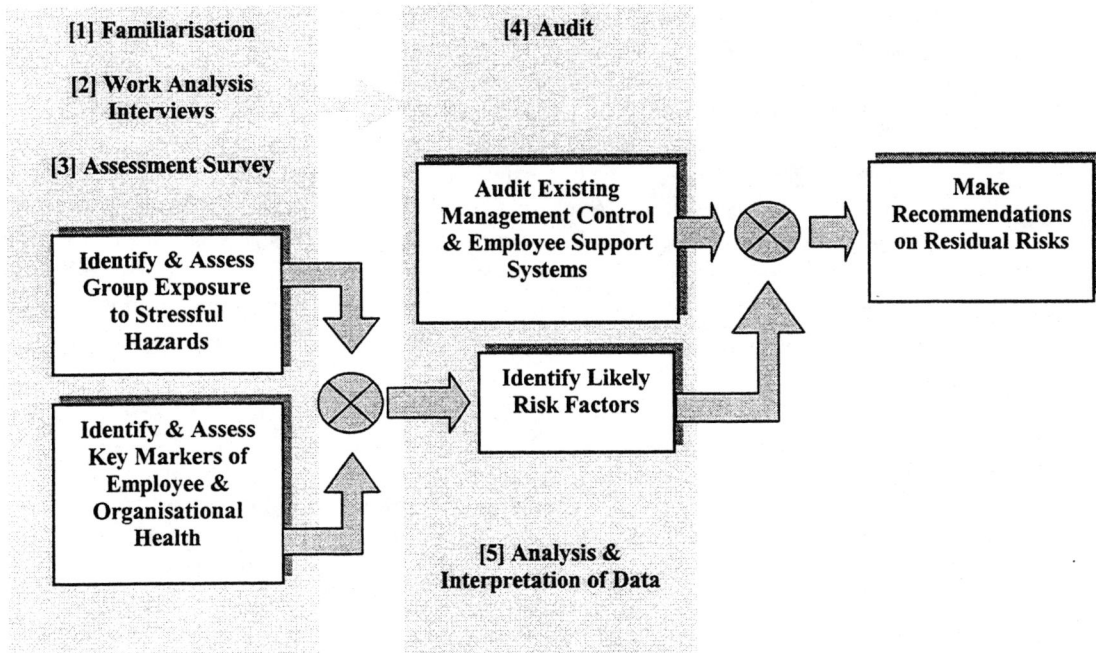

Figure 9: Risk assessment strategy and procedures

3.7.1 STEP 1: Familiarisation

The initial step – familiarisation – is very important. Indeed, its importance in relation to the success of the overall risk management approach cannot be over-stated. It provides the means for 'getting in and getting started', the vehicle for 'getting on', and shapes expectations in relation to 'finishing and getting out'. Careful attention has to be paid to the planning and management of this first step.

Familiarisation has three related objectives. Each is important.

Objectives of the first step: Familiarisation

- Establishing the frameworks, organisation and arrangements that are necessary for the successful completion of the risk assessment: the Steering Group

- Helping the organisation, and its work groups, to get to know the project team and to understand the objectives and nature of the assessment exercise

- Allowing the team to understand the organisation and beginning the collection of the assessment data at the organisational level

---

25

Steering Group: Establishing the frameworks, organisation and arrangements that are necessary for the successful completion of the risk assessment.

One of the first steps in setting up a risk assessment for work stress is to establish a Steering Group to oversee and facilitate the project. It is important that such a Steering Group has both authority and credibility. Both will reflect (a) its terms of reference and (b) its membership. All key stakeholders should be involved in the Steering Group in some way. However, at the same time, the group should be kept as small as possible because it is to be a *working* group. Groups of more than seven or eight people can be difficult to manage.

In the projects completed by the Institute, it has often proved both convenient and effective to organise two different types of Steering Group: an overall project Steering Group – to manage the organisational and strategic issues – working with a more local Steering Group to manage the issues more directly relating to the assessment group chosen. The former groups tended to involve more senior staff, while the latter groups were closer to the "coal faces" and dealt with more technical and process-related issues.

Within each Steering Group, it proved extremely helpful to have a 'project champion', a person who acted as an advocate for the project and also provided the day-by-day contact and information necessary for its successful completion. It was necessary to develop a good working relationship between the project team and the project champion. Problems often occurred in the case study projects when their champions, for whatever reason, moved away. This usually created strategic and operational difficulties until a new and effective champion could be identified and agreed, and a good working relationship established with them.

The Steering Group should serve to both guide and give authority to the risk assessment while maintaining both the organisation's and the employees' sense of involvement. While the exact composition of the Steering Group will need to reflect the organisation's structure and culture, it should represent the interests of all key stakeholders, including the employees.

The composition of the Steering Groups may vary, and did vary, across the case study projects. However, it is important for three groups to be represented:

- Senior and line management

- Occupational health, or health and safety management

- Trades unions, staff associations or employee representatives

Sometimes, specialist management was more appropriately represented by personnel or human resource functions than by those related to occupational health and safety. However, in most of the case studies, the latter group, by reason of their own professional training, had a deeper understanding of what was being attempted, and tended to be more supportive.

A Steering Group has a number of specific tasks to complete: these are presented below.

Steering Group: Tasks

- Representing all interests
- Selecting the work groups to be assessed
- Approving the assessment strategy
- Planning and implementing the educational and marketing strategy for the project
- Monitoring the assessment process
- Discussing and approving progress, including:
- "Signing off" (approving) the survey instrument
- Accepting and discussing the presentation of the assessment data and related recommendations
- Commenting on the assessment report
- Establishing the next step: risk reduction

One of the Steering Group's first tasks is to select the work groups to be involved in the risk assessment, and, in doing so, to provide the evidence to support that choice. It has to approve the strategy to be used. It then has to plan and implement the education and marketing activities that will introduce the risk assessment to those involved, and that will explain the strategy to them, win their trust and encourage their participation.

The Steering Group monitors the progress of the assessment, and acts, as necessary, as a sounding board or discussion forum. It has to approve progress, and, in particular, 'sign off' the final assessment instrument (survey). This survey provides the basis for the formal quantified assessment: those aspects of work and working conditions not included in this part of the exercise are deemed, within the terms of reference of the project, not to be problematic or stressful. The Steering Group may wish to provide others in the organisation with an up-date on the progress of the risk assessment.

The Steering Group also receives the feedback from the assessment, and provides a forum for discussing and exploring these data. This aspect of the project – the translation process – is discussed in more detail in Section 4. The Steering Group may wish to provide others in the organisation with a summary of the assessment data and report, and possibly a commentary on the Report and its recommendations. Whatever, it usually has to decide on the next step – designing and implementing any necessary risk reduction programme (see Sections 4 & 5).

Helping the organisation, and the assessment groups, to get to know the project team, to understand the objectives and nature of the assessment exercise.

It is important that all those involved in the risk assessment within the organisation understand the true nature of the exercise, and how it relates to them. It is also important that the project team has credibility and is trusted. These objectives can most effectively be met through a programme of meetings and discussions, and also by the provision of appropriate information.

The meetings and discussions can be formal or informal as appropriate. Information can be provided by a variety of means, printed (memos, articles in company magazines or newsletters, notices etc) and electronic (e-mails, bulletin boards, web pages, etc.). The provision of printed or electronic information, per se, is usually a passive form of education, and always needs supplementing by more active and participatory exercises –meetings and discussions. Together the meetings, discussions and information dissemination form an educational process that is necessary to facilitate understanding, build trust, and shape appropriate expectations of what can and cannot be achieved. It is effectively a marketing process.

Careful attention has to be paid during the educational process and during the marketing of the project to the appropriateness of employees' perceptions. In particular, attention has to be paid to the natural tendency to see all actions related to stress as being individually-focused and essentially *clinical* in nature. Misperceptions of this kind can not only damage employees' trust in the project and their willingness to participate, but also inappropriately shape their expectations about what can and cannot be achieved.

Getting to understand the organisation and beginning the collection of the assessment data at the organisational level.

One of the objectives of the familiarisation stage is to begin building a model of the work and working conditions of the assessment groups. However, a necessary precursor to model building is to develop an understanding of the organisation: its structure, function and culture. It is particularly important to understand the history of the organisation and the origins of its current culture.

There are a number of methods available to gather the necessary information. However, there is a great deal of variation in both the quantity and quality of information held by organisations. Consequently, the usefulness of the various methods will vary from organisation to organisation. Discussions with key stakeholders may be necessary to get a "feel" for what is available.

Gathering relevant information can be achieved formally by collecting published information such as mission statements, organisational histories, and organisation charts, or less formally through discussions with key stakeholders; managers, employees and trades union representatives. Company reports and recruitment publicity are often useful sources of information. Walk-through observations of workplaces, meeting the people working there, are essential for quickly building an understanding of the organisation and of the assessment groups.

At the same time, it is necessary to review the data and data collection systems that exist within the organisation and that are relevant to the risk assessment. Particularly important will be data on employee absence, both short- and long-term, on labour turnover and transfers within the organisation (and - where available - reasons for leaving), on time keeping, on complaints, accidents and industrial relations problems, and on occupational health referrals.

The importance of such organisational data is not in what it says about particular employees, but partly in:

- The picture it paints of the overall organisation

- The comparisons it allows between sections or departments, functions, sites or levels and grades of employment

Data such as these may provide a justification for choosing a particular work group for assessment.

3.7.2 STEP 2: Work Analysis Interviews

The Work Analysis Interviews were designed to build on the information collected during STEP 1 (Familiarisation) concerning the nature of the work and working conditions of the assessment groups. They are used to develop a model of the work that is 'good enough' to allow the design of the assessment instrument for quantifying employee exposure to the stressors associated with their work and for assessing possible effects on health. Among other things, the interviews were designed to explore potential work-related stressors, and possibly related effects on health, and on health-related and organisational behaviour.

> **Work Analysis Interviews: Focus in case study projects:**
>
> - Building a brief description of the person's work, what they do, why and how, where and with whom
>
> - Identifying its positive aspects and its problems (and sources of stress)
>
> - Exploring how work-related problems are thought to affect the health of those carrying out that work
>
> - Discovering what helps in relation to dealing with work stressors or otherwise coping with them

The interviews in the case study projects were semi-structured and allowed the interviewees an opportunity to talk about their work in their own words. The questions – and other prompts – asked about the common experience and behaviour of the work group rather than that of the individual employee. The objective was to elicit the employees' knowledge by asking them to make 'expert' judgements on their work on behalf of their colleagues in the assessment group.

Technically, this requires situational rather than psychological reasoning; for example, judgements such as 'this aspect of work is problematic because ... ' rather than personal declarations such as 'I feel unhappy with this aspect of work'.

The interviews should be conducted with a structured sample of the assessment group. In the case study projects, the interviews were conducted either individually or in small focus groups, as best suited the organisation. They usually lasted about 30 minutes.

Ideally the necessary focus groups and the individual interviews should be conducted in several phases on a rolling basis. Each phase should cover a more-or-less representative sample of the assessment group, and the process should be continued until no new information is elicited.

The interviewees, however engaged, were asked to talk briefly about the nature of their work – what they did, why and how, where and with whom – its problems, and how work-related problems might affect the health of the work group. The interviews should end on a positive note, asking about the good aspects of work and what helps in dealing with work stressors or otherwise coping with them. The description of the potentially stressful aspects of work and working conditions presented earlier (see also Cox, 1993; Cox, Griffiths and Rial-Gonzalez, 2000) was used in the case study projects to prompt discussion of work and work problems.

3.7.3 STEP 3: The Assessment Survey

Step 3 involves the design and use of an instrument or questionnaire to survey all members of the assessment group to quantify exposure to the main stressors associated with their work and working conditions, and to measure the health of their group. The design of the assessment instrument draws on the information collected during STEP 1 (Familiarisation) and STEP 2 (Work Analysis Interviews). That information should have allowed a model to be built of the work and working conditions of the assessment group. That model should be sufficiently detailed to permit the identification of the major work-related stressors, measures of their likely effects on health and the positive aspects of work.

Design of the Assessment Instrument

The survey instrument should be as short as possible and focused. It should be presented in a format and using language that will be easily understood by the assessment group. The various questions and items that comprise the instrument should be simply constructed, unambiguous and have meaning in relation to the assessment group and the organisation. The questions, items and scales should be designed in accordance with good psychometric practice, and appropriately tested for reliability. The data from each assessment group should also be examined for sensitivity and for evidence of bias.

The survey instrument used in the case study projects was modular:

Survey instrument: Case study projects

- **Module 1**: Job and biographical information

- **Module 2**: Exposure to major work-related stressors

- **Module 3**: Health profile

- **Module 4**: Comments and other information

Module 1: *Job and Biographical Information*
The first module was concerned with two sets of information:

- Information concerning the employee's job
- Biographical information

The former concerned the nature of the employee's job (and grade) within the assessment group and organisation, their length of service, their hours of work and the organisation of those hours, and the nature of their duties. The biographical information largely concerned their age and gender.

There is often a tendency to collect more job related and biographical data than are necessary. This is not only bad practice psychometrically but also, effectively, an invasion of privacy. It should be possible always to justify the inclusion of all the questions in the assessment instrument in relation to the original objectives of that survey.

Module 2: *Exposure to Major Work-related Stressors and the Positive Aspects of Work*
This module was designed to capture employees' expert judgements on the adequacy or otherwise of various aspects of their work and working conditions.

In the case studies, it was presented as a list of items identified for inclusion from the information collected during the first two steps in the assessment process: Familiarisation and the Work Analysis Interviews. The choice of items for inclusion was based on the triangulation of evidence from, at least, three sources among:

- Stake-holder discussions (Familiarisation)

- Walk-through observations (Familiarisation)

- Organisational records (Familiarisation)

- Work Analysis Interviews

The list of items derived from consideration of these different sources was supplemented from the available scientific evidence, where necessary, to provide complete coverage of all possible areas of difficulty as described earlier in this Report (and in Cox, 1993).

The items on this list of potentially stressful and positive aspects of work and working conditions were each associated with a five-point rating scale. Employees were asked to use their knowledge of their work to judge the adequacy of those items on behalf of their co-workers (from 'could not be better' through 'adequate', 'neither adequate nor inadequate' and 'inadequate' to 'unacceptable'). The emphasis was on situational reasoning (see Section 3.7.2).

Questions were also asked about employees' experience of harassment at work. These concerned the source, nature and frequency of harassment.

Module 3: *Health Profile*
Module 3 concerned health as measured by self report. In the case studies, health was broadly defined to include aspects of individual and organisational health.

Case study projects: Measures of health

Self report of:

- Non-specific symptoms of general malaise in relation to feelings of being 'worn out' and of anxiety and tension

- Musculoskeletal discomfort and pain

- Health-related behaviour including sleep duration and quality, smoking and drinking, exercise and diet

- Organisational behaviour including sickness absence, intention to leave organisation, organisational commitment and job satisfaction

---

The measure of general malaise used in the case study projects (see above) was the General Well-being Questionnaire (GWBQ) developed at Nottingham (Cox *et al.*, 1983, 1984: Cox, 1988; Cox and Griffiths, 1995b). This instrument has been used elsewhere in many different studies of work design and management, and there are extensive normative data available. The measures of musculo-skeletal discomfort and pain used (Randall *et al.*, 1998) and of absence, and other organisational behaviours (Thomson *et al.*, 1998) have been described in detail elsewhere. The measures of health-related behaviour were designed to be consistent with those used by OPCS in the survey of the Health of the Nation (OPCS, 1990; Cox *et al.*, 1996). When and where appropriate, these measures were substituted or supplemented by others available within the organisation.

Module 4: Comments and Other Information
The final module was designed to allow employees to comment on the overall exercise or on the design of the assessment survey instrument. It also provided space for employees to add to or elaborate on their judgements on their work and working conditions, or to record extra information about their health.

3.7.4 STEP 4: Audit of Existing Management Control and Employee Support Systems

The audit of existing management control and employee support systems was designed to explore the measures already taken by the organisation, both formal and informal, to deal with stress-related issues. It is necessary to audit these measures and then take them into consideration when subsequently deciding on the residual risk to employees and the recommendations.

The audit used in the case study projects was based on the standard form of enquiry used when auditing health and safety management systems. It explored areas of concern such as:

- Organisational culture and history
- Policy
- Organisation and arrangements supporting policy
- Occupational health and related provision
- Referral systems
- Management and employee training
- Management competence

The audit was conducted through visits to the appropriate parts of the organisation, functional and geographical, interviews and focus groups involving key stakeholders and 'experts' and the collection of written materials and electronically available information.

3.7.5 STEP 5: Analysis and Interpretation of Assessment Data

The data from STEP 3 (the Assessment Survey) were analysed to provide a commentary on the health of the assessment group, the major problems that the group faced in relation to their work and working conditions, the positive aspects of their work, and the likely risk factors for work stress. These data must be interpreted in the light of the other information collected during STEPS 1, 2 and 4, and, in particular, must take proper account of the measures that the organisation has already taken to deal with work stress (STEP 4).

3.7.6 The Analysis Sequence

The analysis was conducted in four basic steps (STEPS 5.1 – 5.4): a discussion of the statistical techniques available to support this sequence is offered in Appendix I.

STEP 5.1: Identification of Stressors

The first step was to use the data from module 2 of the assessment instrument to identify the major stressors reported by the assessment group and to assess group exposure. The question here was one of cut-off: to consider the full range of major problems but not list every individual complaint. A set of guidelines was needed to inform decisions on where the cut-off point should be set.

It has been argued that, because most work stressors are chronic in nature, both the identification of major stressors and the assessment of group exposure can be made in terms of the level of consensus (% agreement) on the presence of the stressor. Therefore identification of major stressors and group exposure was based on the proportion of workers reporting the problem, while taking into account the size of the assessment sample, the number of employees completing the survey instrument and the representativeness of this sub-group. 20% means something different in a returned sample of 20 from one of 200. The greater the size of the assessment group, the greater the response rate and the greater the representativeness of this sub-group, the smaller the % agreement that can be accepted as indicating a significant problem.

Usually, in the case studies, only those stressors that were agreed by the majority of employees (> 50%) were considered, and, in most cases, only those that commanded agreement from three-quarters or more of the assessment group (> 75%) were considered. Attention was paid to the weight of any subsequent legal argument in deciding these cut-offs: "the (vast) majority of employees agreed that this aspect of their work was a problem (stressor)".

Those aspects of work reported as adequate or good by > 50% of the assessment sample should be considered in a similar way, and recommendations should be made to maintain or strengthen these.

STEP 5.2 Health Profile

The second step was to use the data from module 3 of the survey instrument to summarise the health profile of the assessment group. The question here was "how healthy is the group?" in relation to available comparative and normative data.

The health profile of the assessment sample should include a general statement of the overall health status and highlight any particular concerns regarding specific aspects of health. Attention should be drawn, if necessary, to any particular 'at risk' sub-groups, for example, by grade, age or gender, or by workplace.

STEP 5.3 Likely Risk Factors

The third step was to identify likely risk factors by exploring the associations between employees' expert judgements on the adequacy of their work and working conditions and the report of health at the group level. This step combines data from STEPS 5.1 and 5.2. This may be based on statistical analysis or on logical argument. In the latter case, the argument that a stressor is or is not associated with harm to health should be able to stand the test of both logical and legal scrutiny.

The data were analysed to identify which of the major stressors showed evidence of association with negative health outcomes at the group level, and were thus likely to be risks to health. It is important to note that linkage was made at the level of association: it is not possible to tease out and draw precise conclusions about 'cause and effect' in such analyses. Not all the inadequate work characteristics identified will necessarily show an association with health outcomes.

In the case study projects, the main emphasis in the identification of likely risk factors was placed on:

- Non-specific symptoms of general malaise

- Musculoskeletal discomfort and pain

- Health-related behaviour, such as sleep duration and quality, smoking and drinking

- Sickness absence and intention to leave

The statistical strategy used to explore these relationships was based on the use of Odds Ratios (ORs) (see Appendix I). The use of this technique is important because it is consistent with the principles of the risk assessment method developed here. Whereas correlations take the scores of each individual as the data case and establish association at individual level, ORs take group-based frequencies allowing associations to be examined at the level of the whole group.

STEP 5.4 Residual Risk and Recommendations

Having identified the likely risk factors, consideration was given to three factors that might counter the risk to health:

- Existing management control systems

- Employee support systems

- The positive aspects of work

The first two factors were assessed as a result of the audit of management control and employee support systems (STEP 4), while the major positive aspects of work were identified in STEP 5.1 (above). As a result of such consideration, a statement on the residual risk to health, due to work stress, was made.

The balance between the negative aspects of work and working conditions, the positive aspects and measures taken to control stress-related problems and support employees cannot be formulaic, but has to be the subject of professional, legal and scientific judgement.

The final step was the formulation of recommendations on residual risk. In deciding on recommendations, it is necessary not only to identify likely risk factors and residual risk, but also to decide on the priorities for action. This decision may be informed by the statistical analysis of the data, and may involve information on the proportion of workers 'exposed' to the stressor, the strength of the stressor-harm relationship (risk), and the magnitude of the harm. It is likely that any formal calculation based on these dimensions would result in false accuracy and be misleading. Therefore it is suggested that, following common practice elsewhere, these data might be presented diagrammatically. A two-dimensional plot is suggested in Figure 10 below.

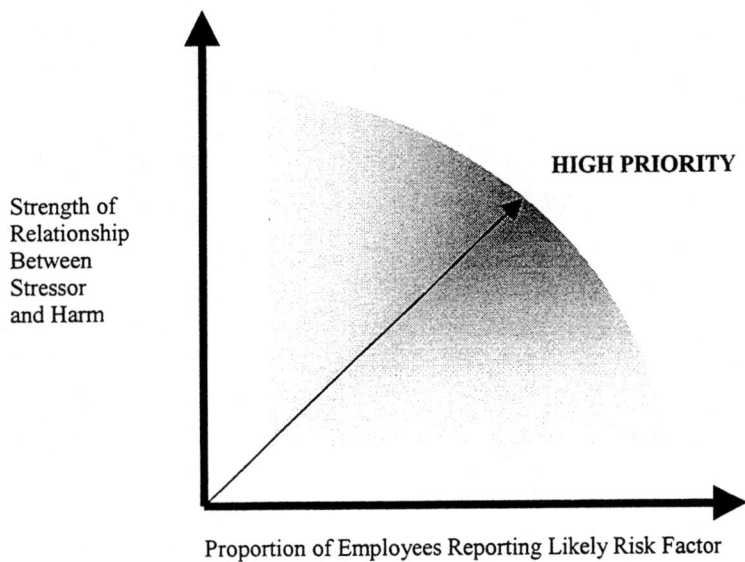

HIGH PRIORITY

Strength of
Relationship
Between
Stressor
and Harm

Proportion of Employees Reporting Likely Risk Factor

Figure 10: Suggested diagrammatic representation of priority of risk factors

It is argued that, in all but extreme situations, the harms caused by exposure to stressors will be broadly equivalent. Plotting magnitude of harm is therefore not necessary. The two dimensional plot is therefore of proportion of workers exposed to the stressor against the strength of the stress-harm relationship. The hypothetical diagonal is thus a dimension of triviality – importance, and the position and closeness of any stressor to this diagonal could inform subsequent decision making. While this plot is not intended to specify exact cut-off points for action, it can be a useful aid to decision making during the translation phase (see Section 4).

Likely Risk Groups

Having established the likely risk factors for the assessment group as a whole, it is then possible to examine if there are any particular 'at risk groups'.

This can be achieved statistically by taking each of the likely risk factors, identifying from the OR calculation who is in the 'response' group for both variables, and running a breakdown on this group's biographical and work details. The question to ask is: do those in the risk group belong to an identifiable sub group, or are they simply a random set of individuals distributed across the whole assessment group? The logic behind this step is that if the people "at risk" are grouped together by some work-related or biographical variable, then it is likely that the factor that they share contributes to the risk.

3.8 ISSUES OF INTERPRETATION

There are two issues that require further comment in relation to the interpretation of the risk assessment data, those of:

- Association

- Generalisation of findings

35

3.8.1 Association

The assessment method operates in terms of *associations* between stressors and health outcomes. This is good enough evidence for the overall risk management process. Re-working the process so that it provides a basis for causal inference may not be feasible in terms of the effort required. One only needs to consider the differential effort required to prove beyond reasonable doubt the effects of asbestos or radiation on health compared to those of job control on cardiovascular disease (see Kristensen, 1996).

The interpretation of such associations must be treated with caution. For example, consider the situation where an association is found between inadequate level of communication with line manager and employees' reports of being worn out. It will remain unclear from the sort of data collected whether the inadequate levels of communication with their line manager cause employees to report feelings of being high 'worn out', or whether feeling 'worn out' causes them to report inadequate levels of communication with their line manager. There might be a third, underlying factor driving both. Associations must be stated and interpreted with caution.

Attempts have been made here to improve the judgements on work and working conditions by making them less subjective, asking employees to use situational reasoning in reaching those judgements (see Section 3.7.2). Employees have been asked about the adequacy of work characteristics, rather than about their feelings of dissatisfaction in relation to those work characteristics.

3.8.2 Generalisation of the Assessment Data

The generalisation of the assessment data and findings can occur at three levels:

- The comparison of raw data

- The comparison of aggregated data

- The comparison of risk factors

The raw data from the assessment can be directly compared across work groups where such comparisons are allowed by the tailoring process. In reality, this most often occurs in relation to the health related data, especially where standard measures have been deliberately included for the purposes of comparison.

Second, the data on stressors and exposure to stressors can be aggregated (grouped) by 'category of stressor'. Suitably weighted, such data can be compared across groups and organisations. For example, two assessment groups might report very different 'organisational stressors' but when the data are suitably weighted it may be clear that for both groups 'organisational stressors' are the main problem area. Conversely, different assessment groups may report essentially the same profile of organisational stressors, but in one it is obvious that they are the main or only problem, while in the other they may be relatively minor compared with much greater problems elsewhere.

Third, the likely risk factors can be compared either directly or by category, or in terms of some underlying organisational pathology identified during the 'translation' process (see also Section 6.4.2).

SECTION 4: TRANSLATION

Section 4 of this Report is concerned with feeding back the assessment information to the organisation, and how such information is related to the exploration and design of any subsequent risk reduction programme. In all the case studies, these activities were found to be crucial. Their importance has resulted in them being conceptualised as a discrete phase of the risk management process: translation. A model of translation based on a medical analogy is described here.

It was believed initially that feeding back the results of the assessment and then deciding on and planning any subsequent interventions would be a straightforward process. However, during the research it became apparent that the related processes by which risk assessment results were used to inform the design, implementation and evaluation of subsequent risk reduction activities were more complex and important than had been anticipated. They represent a distinct phase in the overall risk management process. Discussions with the Finnish Institute of Occupational Health (FIOH) have since lent support to these conclusions. The processes that were involved in bridging the gap between the risk assessment and the risk reduction activities have been termed 'translation processes' (see Figure 11 below).

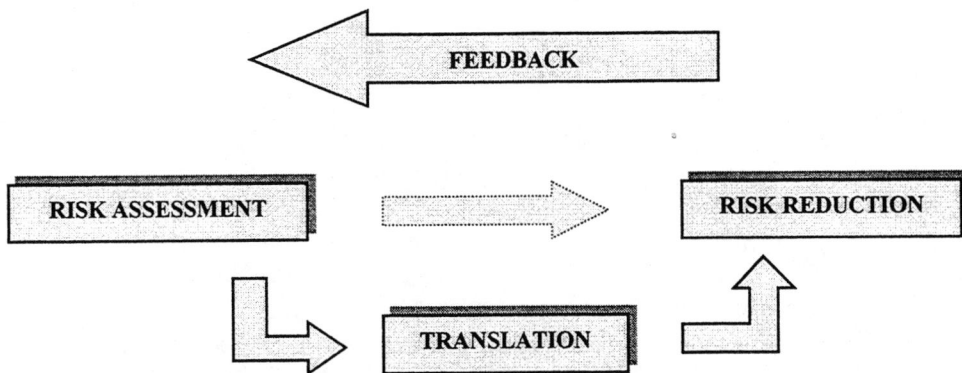

Figure 11: The 'translation processes'

The process of feeding back information was originally conceptualised as a simple link between the phases of risk assessment and risk reduction. No preconceptions existed, except that the discussions would be relatively brief and straightforward. However, in practice, they emerged as rather lengthy and deep. These discussions had a clear structure and progression, and it became obvious that they played a critical part in the success (or otherwise) of the final package of interventions. More specifically, analysis of these discussions indicated that they determined:

- The interventions that took place

- Whether these interventions were seen and implemented as a meaningful, coherent and practical programme of change

- The processes by which interventions were managed, supported and maintained

- The way in which the interventions were evaluated and, ultimately, their success

4.1 THE PROCESSES OF TRANSLATION

4.1.1 Feedback Activities

Feedback varied from case study to case study. However, a number of activities were common across the different studies. The first two centred on facilitating and stimulating the discussion of change:

- Feedback of risk assessment information to the organisation

- Discussion and further exploration of the feedback information

The subsequent activities centred around the planning of actions to tackle the issues that arose from the discussion of feedback information. These were:

- Designing possible interventions to reduce risk

- Prioritisation of feasible actions

- Designing the evaluation

- Marshalling of resources

- Planning the on-the-ground implementation

This section focuses on describing how the risk assessment results were fed back and discussed with organisations, and how this laid the groundwork for the design, implementation and evaluation of risk reduction activities (see Sections 5 & 6). It also presents a description of the 'translation' processes involved.

4.1.2 Managing Feedback to the Organisation

In order to inform and facilitate subsequent change, the information gained during the risk assessment exercise was fed back to the organisation.

In each of the case studies, feedback was focused initially on the Steering Group. The results of the risk assessment were first checked and informally discussed with the project champion, and then with other key stakeholders. This yielded useful information on how the results could be best positioned and best presented. It also allowed the project team to gauge initial reactions and identify outstanding issues. The information was then more formally presented to the Steering Group. This was usually a three-step process. First, the report was introduced to the Steering Group, discussed, and copies distributed for comment. Then those comments were gathered, considered and the Report amended if necessary. It was always made clear that it was the project team who would decide on the necessity and nature of any amendments to the report. Finally, the report was formally handed over to the Steering Group and the organisation.

It was considered crucial, in all the case studies, that feedback on the assessment should *not* be restricted to the Steering Group. Not only was this ethically important, but the promise of wider feedback was often a significant factor in securing employee 'buy-in' to the intervention design and risk reduction activities. Consequently, agreements were usually reached at the outset that a brief summary of the report would be fed back to the assessment group. In many cases, organisations greatly improved on this minimal position (see below).

> **Feedback to employees:**
>
> - Circulation of a summary of the assessment report (sometimes including the Steering Group's response to the results) to the assessment group or to all employees
>
> - Presentation of the assessment report to the assessment group or a meeting of all employees
>
> - Coverage of the assessment exercise in the company newsletter or magazine
>
> - Provision of a special publication (handout, memo, newsletter etc.) on the assessment project

A format emerged for the presentations and reports on the assessment information. This is described below. It had three basic elements.

The first part of the feedback focused on the description of the assessment exercise, placing it in the context of the overall risk management project (and re-iterating some of the key principles). This was also an opportunity to check on expectations and to re-market the overall project. The second part of the presentation focused on the key findings from the assessment. The final part briefly presented the recommendations. Rather than a set of prescriptive actions, recommendations centred on the problems that the organisation should discuss, and on the possible strategies for designing interventions. It began to explore the answer to the question: "What next?". Generally, aids to planning and a schedule for discussions about risk reduction were also introduced at this stage.

> **Translation: Feedback format**
>
> - A 'recap' of the nature of the project and its justification
>
> - A brief review of the risk assessment methodology and activities
>
> - A description of the situation, work and working conditions of the assessment group (to indicate how 'representative' those returning questionnaires were of the assessment group as a whole)
>
> - A profile of its 'health' (broadly defined), compared, where possible, to normative or comparative data without and within the organisation (see Section 3.7)
>
> - An account of the likely risk factors related to working conditions and systems, and 'at risk' groups, with some indication of 'priorities for discussion' (see Section 3.7)
>
> - A review of existing and relevant management control and employee support systems, both formal and informal
>
> - A summary of the recommendations: "what next?"

4.2 IMPLEMENTING TRANSLATION PROCESSES

Prior to the actual research, models of risk management suggested that feedback of results had two simple objectives:

- To inform the Steering Group of the results of the risk assessment, and to stimulate discussion and exploration of the findings

- To determine, agree and justify the need (or otherwise) for reasonably practicable steps to reduce the risk to employees associated with the likely risk factors and hazards

Initially, it was expected that these twin objectives would be met fairly easily within one or two sessions, even allowing for a wide range of political and emotional reactions to the feedback that might slow down and distort the process. What happened in practice was that even two feedback sessions always proved inadequate to the task, somewhat irrespective of the time allowed for them. There were always requests for further meetings. This was largely due to three factors:

- The information load involved and the Steering Groups' need for time and space to digest that information

- The emotional reaction to the information presented and the need to work through immediate 'gut reactions' and to decide on organisationally acceptable 'scripts' to describe the findings

- The political implications of the information presented within the organisation, and the need to consider these carefully

During the series of meetings that evolved, the discussion usually shifted away from the individual risk factors, initially considered one by one and in isolation - as with the items on a shopping list - to an exploration of the linkages between them. Eventually the linkages between the various risk factors and other stressors were used as the bases for discussing and planning action.

Discussing and exploring the linkages between the risk factors and other stressors in order to identify a smaller number of underlying factors led to the Steering Groups producing structured accounts of what was happening – acceptable scripts. These accounts represented interpretations of the risk assessment results within the framework of the Steering Groups' organisational experience and expertise. It produced a more parsimonious model of 'causation'. Often additional information was requested by the Steering Groups to support their models, and, where it was possible and ethical, this was offered by the project team. The structured accounts provided more manageable and economic foundations on which to build risk reduction programmes.

The translation phase illustrates the importance of the Steering Groups and the need for them to be composed of stakeholders with good organisational knowledge.

4.3 MEDICAL ANALOGY

A medical analogy (see Figure 12) proved useful in describing the translation processes. The argument is that the focus of discussion usually shifts away from the detailed and separate risk factors towards the discussion of possible underlying pathologies. The focus shifts away from individual symptoms of occupational and organisational 'ill health' (the risk factors) to the identification and understanding of such pathologies (the underlying processes linking the risk factors). The underlying pathologies become the target of the intervention programme, and in this way, the maximum number of individual risk factors can be dealt with by the minimum number of organisational interventions. In terms of the medical analogy, this process is similar to the way in which a physician will attempt to identify (and subsequently treat) the underlying cause of a variety of presenting symptoms.

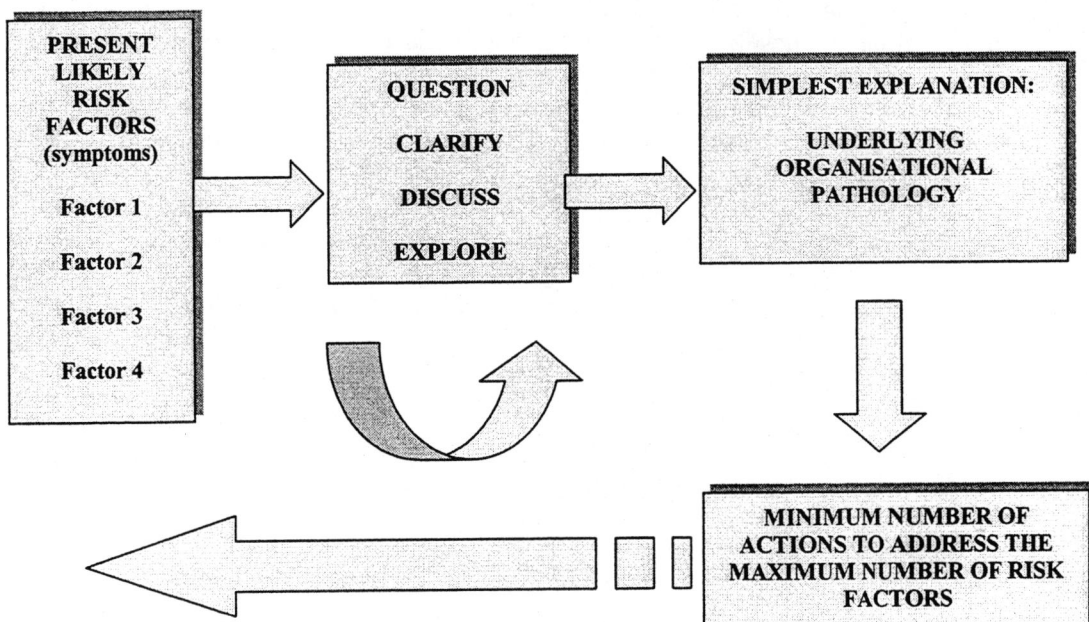

Figure 12: The medical analogy

4.3.1 Different Patterns of Response

Some organisations progressed faster than others towards actual risk reduction. Overall, there appeared to be a negative association between the speed with which the feedback data were discussed and interventions decided, on the one hand, and the likelihood that the organisation dealt with the underlying pathologies - as opposed to dealing with individual symptoms - on the other. In other words, the faster a Steering Group moved to intervene, the more likely it was to focus on the individual risk factors and treat each intervention as a separate issue, producing more of a rag-bag of disparate interventions than a coherent and meaningful risk reduction programme.

There were four problems with such a strategy - or lack of strategy:

- The strategy resulted in a wide variety of interventions aimed at a variety of risk factors that lacked coherence and meaning

- The strategy was therefore difficult to describe and to justify

- It was difficult to manage effectively - either as an organisational project or as an exercise in people or group management

- It did not offer the most effective vehicle for prevention – in terms of the medical analogy, the approach focused on treating the symptoms, rather than the underlying pathology.

4.3.2 Lessons from Elsewhere

Not surprisingly, during the translation process discussions focused on the nature of possible interventions and intervention strategies. At this point, most organisations appeared keen to draw on 'best practice' examples from other organisations. It was not uncommon for the Steering Group to ask the project team for information about what other organisations had tried and how they had proceeded. While examples from other organisations taking part in the overall research and development programme were discussed, the project team was careful not to breach confidentiality nor to present these as prescriptive solutions (see Sections 5 & 6). Rather, they were used to illustrate a number of aids to risk reduction planning (see Section 5). Reference was always made to the scientific literature and to the accumulating experience of the project team.

Sadly, there is not yet a coherent body of 'good practice' information easily available to organisations, although the European Agency for Safety and Health at Work (Bilbao) is collecting and evaluating the information that does exist for dissemination through the Internet. To date, this project offers the largest and most coherent collection of case studies on organisational interventions for work stress framed by a risk management approach.

SECTION 5: RISK REDUCTION

Section 5 of this Report focuses on the design, implementation and management of interventions to reduce risk that were necessary as a result of the assessment exercise. The evaluation of such interventions is dealt with in Section 6. This section is presented in three parts. The first concerns the design of the risk reduction programme and the possible intervention strategies that might be incorporated into that programme. The second part considers the planning and implementation of those interventions, and introduces several aids to planning. The final part looks at the monitoring and management of the risk reduction programme and the feedback of results to the organisation.

5.1 DESIGN

A risk reduction programme should logically begin as an exercise in work and organisational re-design but, in practice, will often need to involve the enhancement of employee support and the development of other occupational health and welfare services. It involves change with people at the heart of that process. Therefore, education and training are powerful tools.

This part of the Report attempts two things. First, it briefly discusses the nature of risk reduction programmes and offers a possible taxonomy. Second, it explores the planning of such interventions and other related processes.

5.1.1 A Taxonomy of Intervention Strategies

The scientific literature on risk reduction in relation to work stress is sparse. Exhaustive reviews of the published literature have failed to produce more than a handful of studies concerned with work or organisational re-design or closely related actions (e.g. Jackson, 1983; Israel *et al.*, 1996). Of course, there are many more studies dealing with individual stress management, but few of them are methodologically sound (Cox, 1993; Parkes & Sparkes, 1998). Apart from these more academic reviews of stress management interventions (e.g., van der Hek & Plomp, 1997; Dollard & Winefield, 1996), much of what is published as advice is too prescriptive. It tends to be limited to didactic prescriptions and recommendations (e.g., Briner, 1997; Kompier *et al.*, 1998), guidance on what amounts to 'good management practice' with some psychological content (e.g., International Federation, 1992, and various publications by NIOSH in the USA) or generic standard recipes for a healthier work environment (e.g. Landy, 1992; Locke, 1976). The European Commission's 1996 'Guidance on Risk Assessment at Work' gives cursory consideration to risk management in Section 5 under the heading 'Actions as a result of risk assessment at work'. It offers only a generic flowchart of options to choose from depending on the results of the assessment. The scientific literature that is available has been discussed in more detail by the authors elsewhere (Cox, Griffiths and Rial-Gonzalez, 2000).

Despite this, taxonomies have been offered of organisational (and individual) interventions for work stress. Several have adopted a three-level model of prevention: primary, secondary, and tertiary. These models are often focused on the individual, not the organisation, and prevention is conceptualised as the avoidance of individual ill-health (so that treatment represents tertiary prevention). There have been two slightly different versions of this taxonomy advanced in the literature on stress management (see Cox, 1993). The first, the more traditional model, distinguishes between:

- Primary prevention as the redesign or re-engineering of work, work systems and technologies, and of work organisations

- Secondary prevention as employee training

- Tertiary prevention as treatment and the subsequent rehabilitation of employees

However, Cox (1993) offered a modified account which takes a more organisational perspective, effectively answering the question "what can the organisation do?". This account makes two important changes to the traditional model:

- It re-defines primary prevention in relation to contemporary stress theory to include employee training

- It refocuses secondary prevention on the organisation's response to employee problems as they arise

Employee training is treated in this model as primary prevention on theoretical grounds. The basic stress equation (Cox, 1993) talks of a critical balance between the demands on people and their ability to cope taking into account needs and resource issues, as well as control and support factors. Reducing stress, so defined, might be achieved by either re-engineering organisational demands, control and support or by increasing the employee's ability to cope (most obviously through training). Training is conceived of as enhancing task related knowledge and skills rather than involving exercises in unsubstantiated, individually focused therapies.

Secondary prevention is conceived in terms of an adequate and timely reaction involving management awareness and training, organisational culture, management and related referral systems, and the availability of appropriate and adequate resources.

5.1.2 Drawbacks of Taxonomies

The existence of such taxonomies might suggest that a particular stress-related problem has an obvious solution by way of a guaranteed and mechanically determined intervention. This has led to the vain hope that organisational interventions might be menu driven, rather like a particular drug being prescribed for a particular disease. If this approach were valid, and it is not, the informed organisation would use a diagnostic tool to identify its main problem and then, consulting the appropriate menu, determine the single intervention (treatment) that would solve that problem. This, of course, is not what happens in reality. Organisations are complex, and their wider environments turbulent. It is naïve to assume that such a menu driven approach would ever be appropriate.

5.1.3 Integrated Solutions to Complex Problems

In all of the case studies, packages of interventions emerged. They were driven as much by the conceptualisation of the underlying organisational pathologies as by the list of individual risk factors (see Section 4). The interventions were tailored to suit the situation of the assessment groups and their organisations. They were usually integrated to provide a meaningful and manageable package. Where this did not happen, interventions were deemed to be less successful.

5.1.4 A Balanced Approach

In all of the case studies, the emphasis was placed on primary and secondary prevention as defined by Cox (1993), and as required by the European and UK legislation. However, in most cases actions were also taken, or had already been taken, to provide enhanced support and welfare for troubled, worried or otherwise stressed employees.

For many reasons - humane, legal, ethical and commercial - it would have been difficult to argue *only* for primary or secondary prevention, forcing the exclusion of tertiary measures. As the project progressed, the notion of *a balanced approach* emerged in which the first consideration was prevention, but attention was also paid to the need for enhanced support and better welfare provision. It was made clear, however, that enhancing employee support *alone* is not recommended as an adequate risk reduction programme.

5.2 PLANNING AND IMPLEMENTATION

Often, in the case studies, the Steering Group felt that its task was complete when it had taken feedback from the assessment, worked through the translation process and determined the design of an intervention programme. This was not so. In reality, its planning activities had just begun. It had then carefully to consider identifying, marshalling and activating the resources required to support the intervention, its implementation and evaluation.

5.2.1 The Role of the Steering Group

The planning, implementation and evaluation of the intervention programme usually remained the responsibility of the original Steering Group. This ensured continuity. However, the Steering Group as originally constituted was not always the most appropriate or most empowered body to carry through the risk reduction programme. In several of the case studies, the Steering Group either changed its membership or, occasionally, delegated responsibility for the intervention to another body. The latter strategy did not usually work as well as the former.

Many of the key issues in planning and implementation were determined by the social and political processes that characterised the organisation. Progress was easier in those cases where the Steering Group had been constituted to include the main stakeholders than in those that had not. The Steering Group was able to act more effectively when it included not only employee representatives, but also:

- Those with the organisational power to decide and act on the outcomes of the assessment

- Those who would be involved in any intervention as managers, trades unionists or functional specialists (i.e., those who could support and maintain the interventions)

- Those who were able to command the necessary resources

While this was not always obvious to the Steering Groups at the outset, it often became so - painfully so in some cases - during the translation and risk reduction phases.

5.2.2 Aids to Planning

Steering Groups often requested help in framing their discussions of likely interventions. In these situations, one or all of the following three 'planning aids' were offered: each represents a conceptual framework for thinking about the design and implementation of risk reduction programmes:

❑ The classical stress equation, as exemplified by the work of Karasek & Theorell (1990), the Michigan School (French, Caplan & van Harrison, 1982), and Cox and his colleagues at Nottingham (Cox, 1993; Cox & Griffiths, 1995b), and presented in terms of a balance between demands and ability to cope considering the level of control and social support available.

Steering Groups often found it useful to analyse likely risk factors and the underlying organisational pathologies in terms of this equation and explore the different ways of re-establishing the essential balance (by re-engineering demands and control, through employee training, and through enhanced support).

❑ A modification of Newman and Beehr's (1979) three-dimensional stress management matrix. This considers [1] the target of any intervention (the individual, their group or the organisation), [2] the strategy used (prevention, timely reaction, or treatment and rehabilitation), and [3] the agency of change (the individual employee, their group, the organisation or external consultants / providers).

This matrix helped Steering Groups to organise their emerging strategies and understand the differences and similarities between the various aspects of those strategies. This, in turn, helped promote the integration and management of the different elements of their intervention programmes. Essentially, this matrix forces questions about "what are we trying to achieve?", "at what level?", "how?", and "whose responsibility will it be?".

❑ The total organisation planning matrix is a three dimensional matrix that considers the time frame for all actions, the part of the organisation / person responsible for them, and the resources needed. Actions are named and conceptualised in terms of their objectives and mechanisms. Reference can be made back to the classical stress equation and to the Newman and Beehr (1979) matrix.

Finally, this total organisation planning matrix prompted more practical thinking; moving planning from a conceptual stage towards practical implementation.

5.3 LEVEL AND COSTS OF INTERVENTIONS

The interventions that emerged in the case studies were generally of three types:

- **Level 1**: Interventions that directly addressed the likely risk factors, individually or through an attack on the underlying organisational pathologies or strengthened the positive aspects of work

- **Level 2**: Actions that were built into on-going initiatives or that modified those initiatives

- **Level 3**: Information that changed existing ways of thinking about employee problems, and the design and management of work

Often a package of interventions was developed that involved both level 1 and 2 interventions and included both preventive and supportive actions (a balanced approach). Such packages were subject to formal evaluation. It was more difficult to evaluate level 3 changes.

The likely cost of any risk reduction exercise was often questioned in advance. In practice, the costs were not as great as was commonly anticipated. Many of the changes that were part of the final package of interventions were themselves relatively low cost, and many could be enacted within existing budgets. In these cases, the risk assessment data had informed and focused existing activities such as organisational development and, in particular, management development and training. Only in a relatively small number of cases were completely new initiatives enacted that were outside existing budget allocations.

5.4 EVALUATION STRATEGY

It was stressed throughout the project that the evaluation of the risk reduction programme should be planned in parallel with the development of the programme itself. This was the case in all the case studies. The evaluations were based on the stated objectives of the programmes in question.

The evaluations were an exercise in applied science. The methodological issues surrounding evaluation are dealt with in the next section.

The evaluation strategy was based on four sources of information:

- An *Intervention Inventory* that assessed the extent and degree of penetration of the intervention actions within the target groups and areas. It measured employees' knowledge of, and involvement in, those actions, and their reactions to them

- A re-distribution of the appropriate parts of the assessment survey to those involved in or affected by the intervention programme and to comparison groups where possible

- Interviews with samples of employees and stakeholders focused on the impact and perceived success of the intervention programme

- Review of available organisational records spanning the period of the intervention programme

5.4.1 Comparisons: Evaluating Organisational Penetration and Impact

In general, evaluation was based on the changes that occurred across the period of the intervention as a factor of its organisational penetration (see section 6). Where possible, the evaluation sought to compare groups or areas that were and were not involved in, or affected by, the intervention programme before and after the intervention. However, it was not often possible to establish or clearly identify such groups or areas. Therefore comparisons were made in terms of the extent to which the interventions penetrated the organisation – the groups and areas involved.

Several comparisons could be made as a result of determining (1) whether or not employees were aware of the interventions, (2) whether or not they were involved in them, or (3) whether or not employees perceived their jobs to be affected by them. These comparisons were arranged in a hierarchical structure:

- Employees who were aware of the interventions *vs* those who did not,

- Among those who were aware, those employees who were involved with the interventions *vs* those who were not,

- Among those who were involved, those employees who perceived their jobs to be affected by the interventions *vs* those who did not.

The amount of data available and their distribution across the potential groups determined which comparisons could be made. In several organisations, the data that the organisation routinely collected and recorded were not sufficient or well enough organised to be used in the evaluation. In nearly all case studies, informal and formal interviews were conducted.

5.5 MONITORING AND MANAGEMENT

In all the case studies, the Steering Groups monitored the progress of the intervention programme and its evaluation in much the same way as they monitored the risk assessment exercise. This was one of their key functions.

Because the risk reduction phase is concerned with change, it is both politically and emotionally sensitive. Both reactions and resistance to change, and the over-enthusiastic or inappropriate promotion of change, had to be monitored and managed. Steering Groups played an important role in smoothing the passage of the intervention programme, and the active involvement and support of the project champion was critical. In one of the case studies, the organisation appointed a small group of Change Managers to facilitate the intervention programme. These operated alongside the Steering Group in explaining and marketing the planned changes, reducing anxieties and rewarding compliance. This group made a noticeable and positive difference.

Monitoring progress is both a formal and an informal exercise, and it needs to exploit all available channels of communication, being alert to rumour and gossip, both of which can powerfully shape employee perceptions of and reactions to change.

5.6 PROCESS ISSUES

There are several important principles that must be honoured in the design and management of any risk reduction programme in order to increase the likelihood that it will prove effective. These are described below.

Design and management of risk reduction programmes - Good practice principles:

- Gain visible and active support of key stakeholders and opinion formers, including senior management and trades unions

- Explain the basis and rationale behind the change to employees and place it in its organisational context

- Provide a realistic vision of what may be achieved

- Involve employees in the change process recognising their expertise

- Encourage employees to own the change process and develop their sense of control over it

- Inform, reassure and support employees during the change process, providing any necessary training at the appropriate time

- Provide regular feedback on how well the change is progressing

---

These principles of good practice reflect the participative approach that characterised the entire project - risk assessment, translation and risk reduction. This was *not* simply an exercise in democracy at work. It is well established that one component driving the experience of work stress is the feeling of not being in control (cf. Cox, 1993). Participation should reduce such feelings, and the method itself should contribute to an improvement in relation to the experience of work stress.

An important part of the process of participation is to educate the employees involved in relation to the planned change, and to offer some vision of what is to be achieved. This vision must reflect the objectives of the intervention programme. The evaluation of the programme provides information on whether or not the vision is being achieved. This information should be fed back to the Steering Group and the employees both during the change process and at the end of the formal evaluation.

5.7 FINAL FEEDBACK TO THE ORGANISATION

The information gained from the evaluation of the intervention programme was fed back to the organisation. As with earlier feedback, it was focused on the Steering Group.

In the case studies, the final feedback process mirrored that for the risk assessment exercise. Results were first checked and informally discussed with the project champion, and then with other key stakeholders. They were then formally presented to and discussed with the Steering Group. The three-step process described earlier was used in the majority of cases. In many cases, further presentations of the overall project were requested, often as a prelude to discussing further work. This work was usually an extension of the overall project to other parts of the organisation, the training of the organisation's staff in the use of the method, or an invitation to continue dealing with specific problems.

It was felt important in all the case studies that feedback on the effectiveness of the intervention programme should not be restricted to the Steering Group. Consequently, agreements were reached, in most cases, that at least an executive summary of the final report would be fed back to the assessment group. Again, in many cases, organisations greatly improved on this.

Feedback, Reports and Case Studies

All participating organisations received detailed reports on their own projects. With the permission of the organisations, six projects have been written up and included in this Report. All the case studies were reported to and discussed with the Health and Safety Executive during the progress of the project. Scientific papers are being published on various aspects of this research and development work.

SECTION 6: EVALUATION AND GENERALISATION

Section 6 of this Report focuses on the methodological issues that surround the evaluation of risk reduction programmes. It reflects in part the arguments between experimental and applied scientists, and between the purist and the pragmatist. Together these arguments have been referred to as the 'Science Wars' (Sardar, 2000). This section is important as it provides the context within which the quality of the evidence provided by this project, and by risk management projects in general, will be judged. It is presented in two parts. The first deals with the design and analysis of evaluation studies in field situations, and addresses the debate over their value. The second part deals with the issue of generalisation. Essentially, it asks in what ways can a very context dependent method provide general lessons.

6.1 SCIENCE OF EVALUATION

The science of evaluation needs to be adaptable. This is because the exact form of any evaluation will be affected by factors such as:

- The nature of the action or situation being evaluated
- The context in which the action or situation occurs and is evaluated
- The use to which that evaluation will be put

In the artificial world of the laboratory where perfect control can be exercised by the scientists involved, an adequate evaluation of a manipulation or intervention equates to the practice of the experimental method. However, in most situations outside the laboratory the necessary level of control is neither practically, nor ethically, possible. In such cases, the methodology of evaluation can only approximate to the experimental method (quasi-experimentation) and will often fail to provide the crucial test of causality sought by most 'pure' scientists.

A dilemma immediately arises: if the ideal is not possible, is it worth accepting the next best thing? To many pure scientists, isolated from the real world pressures to act, the answer can be "NO". To the applied scientist, the ideal is a goal to be aimed for, not a cross on which potentially useful data should be 'crucified'. All information that may promote our ability to solve pressing problems has to be collected and considered as carefully as possible in its social and organisational contexts. The real challenge within the case studies was to adapt and create evaluation methodologies that gave useful information as to the effectiveness of the various interventions and that facilitated further progress.

Cook and Campbell (1979) have discussed the science of quasi-experimentation – experimentation where laboratory levels of control are not possible– in some depth in their seminal book of that name. There are several characteristics of quasi-experimentation that are worth noting in relation to the design of evaluation studies in real world situations. These are discussed below.

Essentially, the whole design issue is an exercise in creative logic; the goal being the ability to draw 'good enough' conclusions about the effectiveness of imposed (or naturally occurring) change against a turbulent organisational background. 'Good enough' conclusions, as their name implies, are not perfect statements of causal relationships: they are suggestions, of varying strength and generalisability, about associations between actions and outcomes. They often include some degree of expert judgement, and this must be honestly and conservatively given. Those that object to the inclusion of this type of evidence in an evaluation study must think carefully of their acceptance of similar processes when they consult their general practitioner with regard to their health or any number of other experts whose judgement is relied upon to make decisions in everyday life. Good enough conclusions may also be context dependent, and recognition of this fact places them squarely in the realm of post-normal science (Sardar, 2000).

6.2 DESIGNS AND MEASURES

Evaluation designs must involve sensible comparisons that bear on the actions or events being evaluated and on the context for those actions and evaluations. Multiple and structured comparisons prove more powerful in the generation of 'good enough' conclusions than single comparisons.

Evaluations and measures are of two types. They can be:

- Process based (*what and how things happened and issues of compliance*)

- Outcome based (*what the result was; the difference that was made*)

A consideration of the relative value of these two types of measure has to take into consideration the design of the study in relation to the issue of comparisons (see above).

Single outcome-based measures taken after an action or event offer little information of value towards a 'good enough' conclusion. Slightly more information is offered in this sort of situation by 'process-based' measures. Even so, their value is limited. Outcome-based measures taken *before and after* an action or event offer slightly more information, especially about change, and their value may be enhanced if they are combined with process-based measures. Better still is the bringing together of before-after comparisons with those among groups that are more or less affected by the actions or events. Here the organisational penetration of the intervention may be treated as an independent variable or co-variate. As described earlier in section 5.4, in the case studies organisational penetration was assessed hierarchically allowing for three meaningful sets of comparisons: first, according to the level of awareness, second, according to the level of involvement, and, third, according to the degree to which the job was affected. The lowest level of penetration was 'not aware' while the highest level of penetration was 'aware, involved and job affected'.

An important point here is that added value may be achieved towards a 'good enough' conclusion from sensibly combining different types of measure and by not focusing entirely on outcome-based measures.

6.3 SAMPLES AND POPULATIONS

It must be made clear whether the evaluation is based on a sample drawn from a larger population or whether it is based on a population in its entirety. The explicit definition of all samples and populations is important. These issues have implications for the statistics employed, how the results are interpreted, and how the results are generalised (see Section 6.4).

Much of experimental science is based on sampling from a larger population so that the study is manageable, and the method of sampling chosen is such that the results of the study-on-a-sample might be generalised to the larger population. This strategy is often focused on macro groups –if not people-in-general– on the assumption that there are fundamental and somewhat simple rules of behaviour that can be applied at a high level of generality across all situations. This is a very pervasive, but erroneous, assumption within the psychological sciences.

There are two common problems with this approach. First, it is likely, from the available evidence, that human behaviour is context dependent (driven by any number of factors that vary across specific situations) and complex. Consequently, simple fundamental rules either do not exist, or will be so simple as to be useless in predicting and managing real world situations. It is clear from studies in chaos and complexity that even if simple rules of behaviour can be sustained, their combination usually produces situations that are unpredictable. Second, in many experiments insufficient attention is paid to sampling issues and, as a result, many of the generalisations that are made are questionable and may falsely inform the assumption of simple rules of behaviour.

In contrast to laboratory-based science, field (applied) science is more concerned with particular situations and specific groups and problems rather than with people-in-general and simple rules of behaviour. This influences the nature of applied studies with regard to samples, populations and the choice of sampling strategy. It also influences the choice of statistical tests, the application of these tests and the interpretation of the results gained. It constrains generalisation, by definition, but this is not a prime issue for many applied situations.

The limitations of the design used must be carefully considered. The threats to causal inference must be identified and understood in relation to the use of statistics, the formulation of conclusions, the caveats placed on those conclusions and the extent to which they might be generalised.

6.4 GENERALISATION

The current project is heavily contextualised in terms of its objectives and its deliverables. However, the issue of generalisability has been considered (below) at three levels:

- Individual case study results

- The generalisation of the data from these case studies

- The transferability of the framework and processes involved

6.4.1 Individual Case Studies

The project has examined the success, or otherwise, of both risk assessments and subsequent interventions across many case studies. The results have been presented separately, and useful information can be drawn from each study (see Sections 9 and 10).

6.4.2 The Generalisation of Case Study Data

Although the results from the case studies are context dependent (valid within the study population and its organisational setting), they can also be generalised. Generalisation of the risk assessment data may occur at three levels (see also Section 3.8.2):

- Comparison of basic data relating to hazards and health 'outcomes'

- Comparison of likely risk factors (across companies and sectors)

- The grouping of the hazard data by the categories suggested in Cox (1993), or by factor analysis or similar techniques, to produce a higher level of profiling

Further, it may be possible formally to generalise results using statistical techniques such as meta-analysis. Thus, an overall commentary will provide an outline of the major risk factors identified in the risk assessments for work stress.

Initial findings suggest, for example, that common risks factors include those not very strongly emphasised in the literature on occupational health (e.g. poor communication with senior management, lack of adequate consultation processes, intimidation and harassment, inadequacy of feedback and appraisal systems). This is one advantage of using a context-based, tailored approach, where assessment instruments are designed for, and in consultation with, each organisation, rather than using imposed 'off the shelf' packages (see Section 6.4.3).

Although the results of each case study intervention are context dependent and valid within the specific work group and its organisational setting, general lessons can be learnt. What can be provided is a commentary on the general feasibility of various types of intervention, evidence that they work, and an outline of the nature and breadth of possible interventions.

6.4.3 Transferability of the Framework and Processes

As part of the requirement to undertake risk assessments and evaluate interventions, the Institute has developed a practicable framework and supporting processes and instruments (technology). The tailored assessment has been found to be the strength of this approach by all of the organisations involved. They have, by and large, rejected the alternative approach based on the imposition of standardised questionnaires, usually at a distance, which cannot deliver the level of detail required to inform the sensible development of a subsequent risk reduction phase. For much the same reasons, they have also questioned the usefulness of addressing the whole organisation at once and as if a single homogenous entity. There is a growing dissatisfaction with these alternative approaches that, in any case, are not always sympathetic to the spirit of the recommended consultation processes[5].

---

[5] HSE (1996) *A Guide to the Health and Safety (Consultation with Employees) Regulations.*

SECTION 7: LEARNING POINTS

This section of Part I of the Report provides a commentary on some of the main process learning points that arose during the development work and in the case studies. Others are discussed in more detail in the six case studies presented in Part II of the Report (Sections 9 and 10).

7.1 PROJECT CHAMPIONS: KEY PLAYERS

In all six case studies, the project champion was either an occupational health physician or a health and safety manager. It became clear that the risk management approach appealed more to these groups than it did to human resource or personnel managers. All the project champions were enthusiastic and supportive of the risk management approach. Their dedication to and day-to-day involvement in the projects proved crucial, particularly in providing a reliable contact point within the organisation and in ensuring that the necessary procedures were properly carried out.

Despite the enthusiasm shown by project champions it was necessary to ensure that they were fully briefed about the risk management approach, its logic, process and procedures. It was also important to ensure that their expectations were consistent with those of the project team.

7.2 SENIOR MANAGERS: SUPPORT AND SHARED UNDERSTANDING

It was always necessary to obtain the full understanding and support of senior managers. Their support had to be secured at the start of the project and made both visible and tangible.

Usually, the support of senior managers was gained with the help of the project champion. The project began with a series of formal presentations by the project team at which some, or all, senior managers were present. These presentations were designed to explain and sell the project: a number of different arguments were developed to persuade senior managers to buy into this research and development work (see Box below). Establishing the link between good health and good business was important.

Senior managers were encouraged to raise any concerns and discuss expectations with the project team so that their questions could be answered. It was important, at this stage, that their expectations were realistically shaped and, on occasions, constrained.

7.3 'TERMS AND CONDITIONS' DOCUMENT

The project team saw the need to formalise the process of agreeing the project with the organisation. When senior management had bought into the project, and it was clear that it would proceed, the organisation was asked to sign up to a 'Terms and Conditions' document. Although this had no legal status, the discussion of its content and the act of signing ensured that the organisation and the project team were working within the same framework. In particular it ensured that senior managers were committed to act upon the results of the risk assessment, and to move into designing and implementing the risk reduction programme.

> **Arguments developed for selling the risk assessment to senior management:**
>
> - Improving the health and satisfaction of the organisation's employees (the *humane* sell)
>
> - Meeting legal requirements to assess all risks to employee health and helping to defend against future litigation (the *legal* sell)
>
> - Selling 'good health is good business' at the individual level: promoting employee health to improve their availability for work and the quality of their work
>
> - Selling 'good health is good business' at the organisational level: improving employee health to reduce sickness absence, insurance costs, and to improve company image
>
> - Selling 'good management practice': conducting a risk assessment to provide good management information for organisational and management development

7.4 STEERING GROUPS

Ideally, the Steering Groups should involve or represent all key stakeholders, including senior and local managers, union representatives and members of the assessment group (see Section 3.7.1). The Steering Group should be well balanced and remain small enough to be an effective working group. This was not always achieved in practice. Discussions over the composition of the Steering Group often exposed the internal politics of the organisation, and, on several occasions, it proved challenging to the project team to ensure that the group was well balanced. Failure to achieve a reasonable composition for the Steering Group always threatened the credibility and perceived independence of the assessment exercise, and thus the success of the overall project.

7.5 CHOOSING THE GROUP TO BE ASSESSED

Steering Groups often had clear views about the groups that should be assessed, usually because they were widely held within the organisation to be 'at risk' from work stress. The project team's task was often to challenge these ideas and to ask for evidence to support commonly held views about being 'at risk'.

Two key factors in determining the success of an assessment proved to be:

- The homogeneity of the assessment group and of their geographical location

- The resources that were available to support the assessment both at organisational and group-levels

There were often local political issues underpinning the choice of the assessment group. For example, one of the assembly operations assessed in a company in the north of England was part of a larger site that included another somewhat similar operation. From informal discussions with the project champion, it became apparent that the former was perceived by its employees as the 'poor relation' to the latter and with some justification. The latter was based in more pleasant and better equipped surroundings. One of the reasons for choosing the former operation for the assessment was to demonstrate the organisation's concern for its workforce.

7.6 MARKETING THE PROJECT

The way in which the project was marketed within the organisation, and, in particular, to the assessment groups in question, proved crucial to its success.

It became custom and practice to work with the project champion and the Steering Group to identify the full range of media and methods available for explaining and selling the project. It always proved important to decide which would be the most suitable for the different groups involved, and which would give the project the highest and most appropriate profile. The six case studies presented at the end of this Report adopted quite different marketing methods.

One case study involved a presentation by the project team on aims and objectives to all members of the assessment sample in an interactive session. This was supported by the distribution of a handout. This was the most suitable method where members of the assessment group were sceptical about the aims of the project and mistrusting of their management. It allowed the project team the opportunity directly and publicly to address the group's concerns. In other case studies, the project was marketed by means of:

- Briefing notes sent by internal mail

- Memos sent via electronic mail

- Presentations to health and safety representatives to be 'passed down' to the assessment groups

- Articles in the organisations newsletter (or similar)

The content of the marketing material – the descriptions offered and the arguments used - was always carefully considered. Besides offering an honest and non-threatening account of the assessment exercise, material had to be user-friendly and accessible and had to guarantee confidentiality.

An important lesson learnt from one of the case studies was that the marketing material should be addressed directly to each employee in the assessment group and not to a job title. Not only did this personalise the approach and encourage a sense of involvement, but it occasionally minimalised errors and gaps in communication. In the case study mentioned above, the structure of the shift pattern used by the organisation meant that while several people shared a job title, only one received the memo marketing the project. There was no overlap in the changeover between shifts and information on the project was not passed on.

7.7 PROJECT NAMING

The amount of time spent discussing the naming of the project and its subsequent importance to the success of the project was surprising. Although most organisations were attracted to the project because it offered knowledge of how to manage work stress, most then proved nervous of labelling it in that way. Three reasons were offered:

- Labelling the initiative as a 'stress' project would suggest an individual and clinical approach to most employees rather than a focus on work and working conditions

- Stress was too political and emotional an issue

- The organisation (or assessment group) would be labelled as 'stressed' whatever the outcome and this sort of publicity could be damaging both internally and externally

In most cases, the projects were labelled in a way that suggested that they were associated with routine health and safety activities or other existing and non-controversial projects. Often an informative but neutral title was used. 'Work and Well-being' was a frequent choice.

7.8 BARRIERS AND FACILITATORS

Risk management has to work against a backdrop of change and development. Barriers to progress can arise from insufficient resources, or a failure to empower the project sufficiently. Other less obvious underlying factors can hamper effective risk management. Many are bipolar: the flip side of the argument being that these factors, in a more favourable state, can facilitate risk management.

These barriers and facilitators have the potential to impact upon a number of stages of the risk management process. However, their impact was felt most during intervention design and subsequent implementation. The project team encountered a number of such factors. Some of the most influential and important included:

- Level of anxiety about the future of the organisation or of the specific work group

- Geographical spread of the assessment group and the effectiveness of the communication links across that group

- Changes in management personnel, structure, or 'culture' particularly relating to the project champion and Steering Group

- Changes in business goals and strategy

- Re-structuring of the organisation or its activities

- Changes in staffing levels

- Variation in local circumstances and working conditions affecting the assessment group

- Opportunities for natural or deliberate variation in the implementation of risk reduction across the assessment group

- Amount of management driven change occurring separately from the risk management activities

Two other important factors also impact upon the evaluation of the interventions. These are:

- Employees' awareness of risk reduction (including their involvement in risk reduction)

- Employees' reactions to the interventions

The importance of these two factors was discussed in Section 5.4.

7.9 COMPLETION

Despite their declared intentions to complete the whole risk management project, some organisations were reluctant to engage in the process of change necessary for effective risk reduction. Fear of costs or political turbulence dominated the thinking of some members of Steering Groups. Interestingly, the economic fears were more easily overcome than the political. Most risk reduction exercises were not very costly. Political fears were often overcome by senior management taking ownership of the programme or by pressure from the trades unions.

At a more operational level, insufficient resources were often allocated by organisations to support the evaluation exercise, and that exercise was not sufficiently empowered within the organisation, again unless senior management had taken ownership. Both of these shortcomings can contribute to a failure effectively to evaluate the risk reduction programme.

There has been much interest expressed, across Europe and in the USA, in the process and results of this research project. We hope that this work will, when appropriately disseminated in academic and professional conferences and publications, contribute to the further development of knowledge and theory in this important area.

We do hope that stress management will be increasingly subsumed under 'good management' practice and organisational development principles (Landsbergis and Vivona-Vaughan, 1995). Stress management is good management. Good management is stress management.

SECTION 8: REFERENCES

Bailey, J.M. & Bhagat, R.S. (1987) *Meaning and measurement of work stressors in the work environment*. In S.V. Kasl and C.L. Cooper (Eds.) Stress and Health: Issues in Research Methodology. Chichester: Wiley.

Bate, R. (1997) *What Risk ?* Oxford: Butterworth-Heinemann.

Beehr, T.A. (1995) *Psychological Stress in the Workplace*. New York: Routledge.

Borg, M.G. (1990) Occupational stress in British educational settings: A review. *Educational Psychology*, 10, 103-126.

Bosma, H., & Marmot, M.G. (1997) Low job control and risk of coronary heart disease in Whitehall II (prospective cohort) study. *British Medical Journal, 314*, no. 7080.

Brief, A.P., Burke, M.J., George, J.M., Robinson, B.S. & Webster, J. (1988) Should negative affectivity remain an unmeasured variable in the study of job stress? *Journal of Applied Psychology, 73*, 193-198.

Briner, R. (1997) Improving stress assessment: Toward an evidence-based approach to organizational stress interventions. *Journal of Psychosomatic Research, 43*, 61-71.

Calman, K. (1993) *Hospital doctors: training for the future. The report of the working group on specialist medical training*. London: Health Publications Unit.

Cartwright, S. & Cooper, C.L. (1996) Public policy and occupational health psychology in Europe. *Journal of Occupational Health Psychology, 1*, 349-361.

Chen, P.Y. & Spector, P.E. (1991) Negative affectivity as the underlying cause of correlations between stressors and strains. *Journal of Applied Psychology, 76*, 398-407.

Control of Substances Hazardous to Health (Amendment) Regulations (1990). Statutory instrument no. 2026. London: HMSO.

Cook, T. D., & Campbell, D. T. (1979) *Quasi-experimentation: Design and Analysis Issues for Field Settings*. Chicago: Rand McNally.

Cooper, C.L. & Marshall, J. (1976) Occupational sources of stress: A review of the literature relating to coronary heart disease and mental ill health. *Journal of Occupational Psychology, 49*, 11-28.

Cox, S., & Tait, R. (1998) *Safety, Reliability and Risk Management*. Oxford: Butterworth-Heinemann.

Cox, T. (1978) *Stress*. London: Macmillan.

Cox, T. (1988) *The psychobiology of stress and health*. In S. Fisher and J. Reason (Eds.) Handbook of Cognition and Health. Chichester: Wiley and Sons.

Cox, T. (1993) *Stress Research and Stress Management: Putting Theory to Work*. Sudbury: HSE Books.

Cox, T. & Cox, S. (1993) *Psychosocial and Organisational Hazards. Monitoring and Control.* Occasional Series in Occupational Health, 5. Copenhagen: World Health Organisation (Europe).

Cox, T. & Ferguson, E. (1994) *Measurement of the subjective work environment.* Work and Stress, 8, 98-109.

Cox, T. & Griffiths, A.J. (1995a) *The assessment of psychosocial hazards at work.* In M.J. Shabracq, J.A.M. Winnubst and C.L. Cooper (Eds.) Handbook of Work and Health Psychology. Chichester: John Wiley and Sons.

Cox, T. & Griffiths, A.J. (1995b) *The nature and measurement of work stress: theory and practice.* In Wilson, J. and Corlett, N. (Eds.) The Evaluation of Human Work: A Practical Ergonomics Methodology. London: Taylor and Francis,

Cox, T., Griffiths, A. J., Barlow, C. A., Gustafsson, E. & Cox, S. (1996) *Work-related Stress in Manual Workers: A Heavy Load.* London: UNISON.

Cox, T., Griffiths, A. J. & Rial-Gonzalez, E. (2000) *Research on Work-related Stress.* Report for the European Agency for Safety and Health at Work. Luxembourg: Office for Official Publications of the European Communities.

Cox, T., Thirlaway, M. & Cox, S. (1984) *Occupational well-being: sex differences at work.* Ergonomics, 27, 499-510.

Cox, T., Thirlaway, M., Gotts, G. and Cox, S. (1983) The nature and assessment of general well-being. *Journal of Psychosomatic Research, 27,* 353-359.

Council of the European Commission (1989) *Council Directive 89/391/EEC:* The Introduction of Measures to Encourage Improvements in the Safety and Health of Workers at Work. Luxembourg: European Commission.

Department of Health (1986) *Hospital Medical Staffing: Achieving a Balance.* London: DHSS.

Department of Health (1991) *Junior Doctors: The New Deal.* London: DHSS.

Dollard, MF & Winefield, AH (1996) Managing occupational stress: a national and international perspective. *International Journal of Stress Management, 3,* 69-83.

Einhoven, H. J., & Hogarth, R. M. (1981). Behavioural decision theory: processes of judgement and choice. *Annual Review of Psychology, 32,* 53-88.

European Commission Directorate General V (1996) *Guidance on Risk Assessment at Work.* Luxembourg: European Commission.

FIET [International Federation of Commercial, Clerical, Professional and Technical Employees] (1992) *Resolutions adopted by the 22nd FIET World Congress* (San Francisco, 1991). Geneva: FIET.

French J.R.P., Caplan, R.D & Van Harrison, R. (1982) The Mechanisms of Job Stress and Strain. Chichester: Wiley.

Frese, M. & Zapf, D. (1988) *Methodological issues in the study of work stress: Objective vs. subjective measurement of work stress and the question of longitudinal studies.* In C.L. Cooper and R. Payne (Eds.) Causes, Coping and Consequences of Stress at Work. Chichester: John Wiley and Sons.

Ferguson, E. & Cox, T. !993) Exploratory factor analysis: A users' guide. *International Journal of Selection and Assessment, 1*, 84-94.

Gardell, B. (1982) Work participation and autonothis: A multilevel approach to democracy at the workplace. *International Journal of Health Services, 12*, 31-41.

Goodman, L. A. (1978) *Analyzing Qualitative/Categorical Data.* Maryland: Abt Books.

Gotts, G. & Cox, T. (1990) *The General Well-Being Questionnaire. The Manual.* Sutton Coldfield: Maxwell and Cox Associates.

Griffiths, A.J. (1998) Work-related illness in Great Britain. *Work and Stress, 12*, 1-5.

Griffiths, A.J., Cox, T. & Stokes, A. (1995) Work-related stress and the law: the current position. *Journal of Employment Law and Practice, 2*, 93-96.

Health and Safety Commission (1992) *Management of Health and Safety Regulations* (1992) London: HMSO.

Health and Safety Commission (1999) *Management of Health and Safety at Work: Management of Health and Safety at Work Regulations 1999, Approved Code of Practice and Guidance.* Sudbury: HSE Books.

Health and Safety at Work etc. Act (1974). London: HMSO.

Health and Safety Executive (1995) *Guidance for Employers on Work Related Stress.* London: HMSO.

Hennekens, C. H. & Buring, J. E. (1987) *Epidemiology in Medicine.* Boston: Little Brown.

Hernberg, S. (1994a) 20th Anniversary Issue: Editorial. *Scandinavian Journal of Work, Environment and Health, 20*, 5-7.

Hernberg, S. (1994b) New epidemics in occupational health. *Scandinavian Journal of Work, Environment and Health, 20*, 309-311.

Hiebert, B. & Farber, I. (1984) Teacher stress: A literature survey with a few surprises. *Canadian Journal of Education, 9*, 14-27.

Hosmer, D. W. & Lemeshow, S. (1989) *Applied Logistic Regression.* New York: John Wiley and Sons.

House, J., Stretcher, V., Metzner, H. & Robbins, C. (1986) Occupational stress among men and women in the Tecumseh Community Health Study. *Journal of Health and Social Behaviour, 27*, 62-77.

Howell, D. C. (1992) *Statistical Methods for Psychology.* Belmont: Duxbury Press.

Hurst, N. W. (1998) *Risk assessment: The human dimension*. Cambridge: Royal Society of Chemistry.

ILO (1992) *Conditions of Work Digest on Preventing Stress at Work, 11 (2)*. Geneva: ILO.

International Federation of Commercial, Clerical and Technical Employees [FIET] (1992) *Resolutions adopted by the 22nd FIET World Congress* (San Fransisco, August 1991). Geneva: FIET

Israel, B.A., Baker, E.A., Goldenhar, L.M., Heaney, C.A. & Schurman, S.J. (1996) Occupational stress, safety and health: Conceptual framework and principles for effective prevention interventions. *Journal of Occupational Health Psychology, 1*, 261-286.

Jackson, S.E. (1983) Participation in decision-making as a strategy for reducing job-related stress. *Journal of Applied Psychology, 68*, 3-19.

Jex, S.M. & Spector, P.E. (1996) The impact of negative affectivity on stressor-strain relations: a replication and extension. *Work and Stress, 10*, 36-45.

Jick, T.D. (1979) Mixing qualitative and quantitative methods: Triangulation in action. *Administrative Science Quarterly, 24*, 602-611.

Johnson, J.V. (1996) Conceptual and methodological developments in occupational stress research. An introduction to state-of-the-art reviews I. *Journal of Occupational Health Psychology, 1*, 6-8.

Johnson, J.V. & Hall, E.M. (1996) Dialectic between conceptual and causal enquiry in psychosocial work-environment research. *Journal of Occupational Health Psychology, 1*, 362-374.

Karasek, R. & Theorell, T. (1990) *Healthy Work*. New York: Basic Books.

Kasl, S.V. (1978) *Epidemiological contributions to the study of work stress*. In C.L. Cooper and R. Payne (Eds.) Stress at Work. Chichester: John Wiley and Sons.

Kasl, S.V. (1981) The challenge of studying the disease effects of stressful work conditions. *American Journal of Public Health, 71*, 682-684.

Kasl, S.V. (1986) *Stress and disease in the workplace: A methodological commentary on the accumulated evidence*. In M.F. Cataldo and T.J. Coates (Eds.) Health and Industry: A behavioral medicine perspective. New York: John Wiley and Sons.

Kasl, S.V. (1987) *Methodologies in stress and health: past difficulties, present dilemmas, future directions*. In S.V. Kasl and C.L. Cooper (Eds.) Stress and Health: Issues in Research Methodology. Chichester: John Wiley and Sons.

Kasl, S.V. (1990) *Assessing health risks in the work setting*. In S. Hobfoll (Ed.) New Directions in Health Psychology Assessment. Washington D.C.: Hemisphere Publishing Corporation.

Kelly, G. A. (1955) *The psychology of personal constructs (vols. 1 & 2)*. New York: Norton.

Kompier, MAJ, Geurts, SAE, Grundeman, RWM, Vink, P & Smulders, PGW (1998) Cases in stress prevention: the success of a participative and stepwise approach. *Stress Medicine, 14*, 155-168

Koopman, P. L. & Pool, J. (1990) Decision making in organisations. In, C. L. Cooper and I. T. Robertson (Eds.) *International Review of Industrial Psychology (vol 5, pp 101-148)*. New York: Wiley and Sons.

Kristensen, T.S. (1996) Job stress and cardiovascular disease: A theoretic critical review. *Journal of Occupational Health Psychology, 1*, 246-260.

Lancaster, R.J., Pilkington, A., & Graveling, R. (1999) *Evaluation of the Organisational Stress Health Audit*. Edinburgh: Institute of Occupational Medicine.

Landsbergis, P.A. & Vivona-Vaughan, E. (1995) Evaluation of an occupational stress intervention in a public agency. *Journal of Organizational Behavior, 16*, 29-48.

Landy, F.J. (1992) *Work design and stress*. In G.P. Keita and S.L. Sauter (Eds.) Work and Well-Being: An Agenda for the 1990s. Washington D.C.: American Psychological Association.

Landy, F.J., Quick, J.C. & Kasl, S. (1994) *Work, stress and well-being*. International Journal of Stress Management. 1, 33-73.

Laufer, E.A., & Glick, J. (1998) *Expert and novice differences in cognition and activity: A practical work activity*. In Y Engestrom and D. Middleton (eds) Cognition and Communication at Work. Cambridge: Cambridge University Press.

Levi, L., Frankenhauser, M. & Gardell, B. (1986) *The characteristics of the workplace and the nature of its social demands*. In S. Wolf and A.J. Finestone (Eds.) Occupational Stress, Health and Performance at Work. Litleton, Maryland: PSG Publications Co. Inc.

Locke, A.A. (1976) *The nature and causes of job satisfaction*. In M.D. Dunnette (Ed.) Handbook of Industrial and Organisational Psychology. Chicago: Rand McNally.

Marmot, M. & Theorell, T. (1988) Social class and cardiovascular disease. The contribution of work. *International Journal of Health Services, 18*, 659-674.

McLean, A.A. (1985) *Work Stress*. Massachusetts: Addison-Wesley Publishing Co.

Morgan, M.G. (1993) Risk analysis and management. *Scientific American, 269*,32 – et seq.

Murphy, L.R. (1984) Occupational stress: A review and appraisal. *Journal of Occupational Psychology*, 57, 1-15.

Murphy, L.R. (1988) *Workplace interventions for stress reduction and prevention*. In C.L. Cooper and R. Payne (Eds.) Causes, Coping and Consequences of Stress at Work. Chichester: John Wiley.

Newman, J. E. & Beehr, T. A. (1979) Personal and organizational strategies for handling job stress: a review of research and opinion. *Personnel Psychology. 32*, 1-43.

Norros, L. (1998) *System disturbances as (a) springboard for development of operators' expertise*. In Y. Engestrom and D. Middleton (Eds.) Cognition and Communication at Work. Cambridge: Cambridge University Press.

OECD [Organisation for Economic Co-operation and Development and the International Programme on Chemical Safety] (1997) *Joint Project on the Harmonization of Chemical Hazard / Risk Assessment Terminology*. Available on the Internet at: http://www.who.ch/programmes/pcs/rsk_term/term_des.htm

OPCS [Office of Population Censuses and Surveys] (1996) *Health Related Behaviour: An Epidemiological Overview*. London: HMSO.

Parkes, K.R. & Sparkes, T.J. (1998) *Organizational interventions to reduce work stress: Are they effective? A review of the literature*. Sudbury: HSE Books.

Randall, R. J., Griffiths, A. J. Barlow, C. A. & Cox, T. R. (1998) *The importance of stress and psychosocial factors in the reporting of musculoskeletal pain: An empirical investigation*. Paper to: 1st International Commission on Occupational Health Conference on Psychosocial Factors at Work. Copenhagen.

Rogers, E.H. (1960) *The Ecology of Health*. New York: Macmillan.

Sardar, Z. (2000) *Thomas Kuhn and the Science Wars*. Cambridge: Icon Books.

Schonfeld, I.S. (1996) Relation of negative affectivity to self-reports of job stressors and psychological outcomes. *Journal of Occupational Health Psychology, 1*, 397-412.

Schott, F. (1992) *Panel comments: work design*. In G.P. Keita and S.L. Sauter (Eds.) Work and Well-Being: An Agenda for the 1990s. Washington D.C.: American Psychological Association.

Scribner, S. (1990) *Manufacturing resource planning*. Paper to: 2nd International Congress on Activity Theory. Lahti, Finland.

Sheffield, D., Dobbie, D. & Carroll, D. (1994) Stress, social support, and psychological wellbeing in secondary school teachers. *Work and Stress, 8*, 235-243.

Spector, P.E. (1987) Method variance as an artefact in self-reported affect and perceptions at work: Myth or significant problem? *Journal of Applied Psychology, 72*, 438-443.

Stansfeld, S.A., North, F.M., White, I. & Marmot, M.G. (1995) Work characteristics and psychiatric disorder in civil servants in London. *Journal of Epidemiology and Community Health, 49*, 48-53.

Stranks, J. (1996) *The Law and Practice of Risk Assessment*. London: Pitman.

Tabachnick, B.G. & Fidell, L.S. (1989) *Using Multivariate Statistics*. New York: Harper-Collins.

Thomson, L., Griffiths, A., & Cox, T. (1998) *The psychometric quality of self-reported absence data*. Proceedings of the International Work Psychology Conference. Sheffield: University of Sheffield, Institute of Work Psychology.

US Department of Health and Human Services National Institute of Occupational Safety and Health (1988) *Psychosocial occupational health*. Washington D.C: NIOSH.

US Department of Health and Human Services National Institute of Occupational Safety and Health (1997) *National Occupational Research Agenda (NORA)*. Available on the Internet at: http://www.cdc.gov/niosh/nora.html

Van der Hek, H. & Plomp, H.N. (1997) Occupational stress management programmes: a practical overview of published effect studies. *Occupational Medicine, 47*, 133-141.

Walker v. Northumberland County Council (1995) *Industrial Relations Law Reports, 35*.

Wang, M., Eddy, J.M. & Fitzhugh, E.C. (1995) Application of odds ratio and logistic models in epidemiology and health research. *Health Values, 19*, 59-62.

Warr, P.B. (1987) *Work, Unemployment and Mental Health*. Cambridge: Cambridge University Press.

Warr, P.B. (1992) *Job features and excessive stress*. In R. Jenkins and N. Coney (Eds.) Prevention of Mental Ill Health at Work. London: HMSO.

Wiegman, O. & Gutteling, J.M. (1995) Risk appraisal and risk communication: Some empirical data from the Netherlands reviewed. *Journal of Hazardous Materials, 10*, 167-178.

PART II

THE CASE STUDIES

SECTION 9: INTRODUCTION TO THE CASE STUDIES

This project concerns the development and testing of a risk management approach to work stress. The focus of the approach is primarily on organisational interventions and primary prevention. The application of such an approach is in itself an organisational intervention to deal with the challenge of work stress.

The application of the risk management approach is illustrated in this Report by six organisational case studies taken from a series of 10 carried out in British private sector companies. Together they cover 11 different occupational groups. This Introduction to the case studies provides an overview of their structure and content.

Part I of this Report sets out and discusses the risk management approach in terms of risk assessment (Section 3), the translation process (Section 4) and risk reduction (Section 5). It also considers the methodological issues surrounding the evaluation of risk reduction programmes (Section 6) and presents some 'learning points' deriving from the development process (Section 7). This Introduction provides the link between Part I of the Report and the case studies (Section 10). It attempts its own 'translation' between the more technical language of the former and a slightly more journalistic style of the latter. The authors hope that this allows the case studies to be both readable and interesting. However, some basic knowledge of the concepts and language of health and safety has had to be assumed. This Introduction should also be read in conjunction with Part I of the Report in order to gain a full understanding of the processes involved in the risk management approach. Reference should be made to this Introduction and the Glossary found at the end of the Report when reading the case studies.

THE STRUCTURE OF THE CASE STUDIES

Each of the case contains six sections:

1. Summary
2. Background
3. Phase I: Risk Assessment
4. Phase II: Translation and Risk Reduction
5. Phase III: Evaluation
6. Learning Points

Together, these sections tell the story of how each project was carried out. The content of these sections is discussed in more detail below. 'Signposts' are included in the case studies so that interested readers can refer to the appropriate information in Part I of the Report. Appendix II also provides a glossary of the technical terms used throughout the Report.

---

1. SUMMARY

Brief information is given about the nature of the risk assessment group and the work they were involved in. The findings from the main phases of the project are outlined.

2. BACKGROUND

This section provides a brief overview of the case study organisation and the type of work carried out by the occupational groups involved in the risk management project: the assessment groups. The relevant organisational history and context are summarised. This includes details about recent events within the organisation, and a description of the organisational culture at the beginning of the project. An account of how contact was made with the organisation is also given, together with details of the project Steering Group. Much of this information was obtained through the Audit of Management Control & Employee Support Systems and an examination of organisational documentation.

3. PHASE I: RISK ASSESSMENT

During this phase of the project, the sources of the stress-related problems were identified and analysed, and likely risk factors for work stress identified.

3.1 PROCESS

The initial steps in the risk assessment process were Familiarisation (Section 3.7.1), the Management Systems Audit (Section 3.7.4), and the Work Analysis Interviews (Section 3.7.2).

Familiarisation involved a number of activities, including the examination of organisational data, discussions with stakeholders and walk-through workplace observations. Building on the information obtained through Familiarisation, the focus moved to the Work Analysis Interviews. These were conducted with a representative sample of employees from each of the assessment groups involved. The Management Systems Audit was usually conducted in parallel with the other activities.

Information from all three activities was used to inform the design of the instrument for use in the subsequent Risk Assessment Survey. This instrument was made up of three main sections: an initial enquiry about the employee and their work, the Work Environment Survey (WES), and a series of scales to measure aspects of occupational and organisational health (Section 3.7.3).

The Work Environment Survey questioned employees about sources of stress largely relating to the design and management of their work and its social and organisational contexts, and about the positive aspects of their work. It was tailored to their particular needs and work context (see Section 3.5 of Part I of the Report, on tailoring the design of the WES).

The scales measuring aspects of occupational and organisational health included coverage of: general well-being, job satisfaction, health related behaviour, the experience of work-related musculoskeletal discomfort and pain, and sickness absence and intention to leave the company.

3.2 ASSESSMENT RESULTS

This section outlines the main findings of the risk assessment. These focus on the likely risk factors for the assessment groups involved and the other major stressors chosen for discussion by the Steering Groups. Most Steering Groups chose to broaden their discussions beyond the list of likely risk factors fed back to them by including some of the other major stressors identified by the risk assessment. These 'other major stressors' were the aspects of the design and management of work that had been identified by the majority of employees in the assessment group as 'inadequate' or 'problematic' but for which there was no strong evidence of a link to health (see Figure 8). In groups where a large number of stressors were reported, a cut-off of 70% endorsement (consensus) was taken. In groups reporting fewer and less serious stressors, this level was adjusted downwards to 50% endorsement.

Summaries of the overall health profile of the assessment groups are also presented (as measured). These profiles indicate the extent of the health problem for those groups, and the urgency of and challenge for any subsequent risk reduction programmes. Judgements about the nature of the health profiles are made by comparing the data to those of other groups involved in similar work or to established normative data. Information gathered during Familiarisation and the Work Analysis Interviews is used to elaborate these findings.

Interventions to reduce risk were largely, but not exclusively, based on altering work design or management in some way. Although the risk management approach focuses on likely risk factors, most organisations also wished to address those aspects of work and working conditions that, although not shown to be risk factors, were reported by the majority of employees as inadequate. Sources of satisfaction were also identified and considered during intervention design.

4. PHASE II: TRANSLATION AND RISK REDUCTION

This section provides information on how the results of the risk assessment phase were fed back to the Steering Groups and 'translated' into interventions to reduce the risk of work stress. It also makes reference to the nature of the intervention programmes and their implementation. It combines the translation and risk reduction stages from Part I of the Report.

The process of translation varied greatly between the case studies. It usually included a prolonged and in-depth exploration of the likely risk factors, and other major stressors, often uncovering underlying organisational pathologies. These discussions - and the structured accounts of the organisational pathologies that emerged - were very important in the design of the risk reduction programmes. A more detailed discussion of the translation process can be found in Section 4 of Part I of the Report.

For each of these case studies, information is given on the 'bespoke' package of interventions that was put into place. Details are also provided about the way in which each intervention was thought to address the problems identified and any underlying organisational pathologies.

5. PHASE III: EVALUATION

This section discusses the nature and results of the evaluation of the intervention package.

5.1 METHOD

The method for gathering data for the evaluation of the risk reduction interventions was similar in part to that used during the risk assessment phase.

The Work Environment Survey was generally shortened to focus on: the likely risk factors, any other major stressors considered, and the positive aspects of work. This allowed a direct comparisons to be made with the original risk assessment data. Organisational and interview data were also collected where possible, and compared to that gathered during the original assessment. The logistics of collecting the data are outlined for each study. The prevailing organisational climate during the intervention and evaluation period is also discussed.

A key aspect of the evaluations was the assessment of the degree to which the interventions had penetrated the organisation in terms of how many employees were aware of them, involved in them, or thought that their jobs had been affected by them. This was achieved using an intervention inventory. Employees used this inventory to indicate their awareness of, involvement in, and reaction to various interventions. These data were used to structure the comparisons at the heart of the evaluation exercise. The various evaluation measures were informed through discussions with employees, management and key stakeholders. The methods used to design the evaluation instruments are outlined in each case study.

5.2 EVALUATION RESULTS

The results from the evaluation phase covered two main issues:

- *Differences between the Assessment and Evaluation Surveys*, in terms of employees' expert judgements on working conditions. These data gave the 'headline' findings on whether work had changed over the period in which the interventions had been in place.

- *Organisational Penetration and Impact (Section 5.4.1)*. 'Headline' (overall or major) differences in health profiles are discussed in this section. However, in order to 'tease out' the real impact of each intervention, comparisons were made according to the organisational penetration of the interventions. Details are given regarding how many employees had been aware of and involved in the interventions, and how many reported that their jobs had changed as a result. Significant differences (see Figure 1) in the health and working conditions are reported for those who were aware of the interventions (*vs* those unaware), for those involved (*vs* those not involved), and for those whose jobs were reported to have changed as a result (*vs* those whose jobs had not changed). Where possible, results drawn from records kept by the organisation are also discussed.

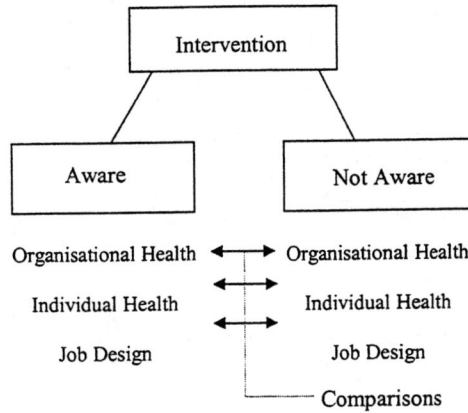

Figure 1: Evaluating the Impact of Interventions

These data are presented in detail for each of the case studies, and a commentary is given on the likely processes underlying the findings.

6. LEARNING POINTS

This final section considers the lessons learned from each case study. It focuses on the challenges faced when applying a risk management approach to work-related stress within real and functioning organisations. These sections should be read in conjunction with section 7 of Part I of the Report.

Practical challenges are discussed in detail. Possible solutions and guidance are offered. Details on methodological challenges are provided throughout the Report.

SECTION 10: THE CASE STUDIES

CASE STUDY 1

CUSTOMER CONTACT STAFF

1. SUMMARY

The project was carried out in the Customer Contact Centre of a large utility firm. The employees involved were those dealing with telephone enquiries from customers (Telephone Billing) and those dealing with written correspondence from customers (Post Billing).

1.1 PHASE I: RISK ASSESSMENT

During June and July 1997, the likely risks to employee health and organisational effectiveness were identified. Employees in both Post Billing and Telephone Billing reported a large number of problems related to the design and management of their work (stressors). Some problems were also evident when the health profile of the group was examined. On average, staff reported being more 'worn out' than was desirable. Many wanted to leave the company and job satisfaction was low. Absence levels were moderate to high, and a relatively large proportion of employees reported work-related musculoskeletal pain. These poor organisational and individual health profiles tended to be associated with several of the following likely risk factors and stressors:

- Unrealistic performance targets, and a lack of praise and recognition
- Poor communication with senior management
- Slow movement of information around the organisation
- Having to deal with multiple tasks of equal importance
- Lack of support from, and poor availability of, line managers
- Lack of time to complete tasks
- Inadequate time for breaks during the day

1.2 PHASE II: TRANSLATION AND RISK REDUCTION

Feedback of the results of the risk assessment dove-tailed with ambitious plans for change announced by the organisation for the Customer Contact Centre. The Steering Group produced an extensive package of interventions that targeted the identified risk factors, the stressors and their underlying pathologies. The interventions included:

- Changes in the management of performance targets
- Instigation of more regular, structured and purposeful team meetings
- Measures to improve organisational communication
- Introduction of new training initiatives
- Introduction of quality monitoring
- Introduction of 'Best Practice' guidelines and changes in working procedures
- A review and updating of staffing levels to meet increased public demand
- Formal break-taking arrangements
- Changes in IT systems and introduction of new systems

1.3 PHASE III: EVALUATION

The evaluation phase was carried out in November 1998. Although some problems remained, a number of positive findings emerged:

- There was a high level of awareness of a number of interventions

- Staff reported that many of the interventions had made their work better

- When compared to 1997, there was a drop in the number of staff reporting the stressors and risk factors

- There was evidence of more positive well-being among those who indicated that the interventions had improved their work

- Absence was reduced and remained steady at around 5%

Given the initial problems identified in the risk assessment and the demanding nature of the work being carried out by the customer contact staff, these results were received as encouraging. However, bearing in mind the rapidly changing nature of work in the Customer Contact Centre, it was recommended that stressors remaining at the evaluation stage be monitored and further attempts made to tackle them.

2. BACKGROUND

The utility company involved in the project provides a service for domestic and commercial customers among a population of 5.5 million throughout a region of England. The company was privatised in the late 1980s and since then its customer service has been governed by a number of regulatory standards. Changes in the way its services are delivered and paid for have resulted in increased demand for customer contact service staff over recent years. The company was aware that customer contact staff were working under immense pressure to deal with the growing and rapidly changing demands placed on them.

At the time of the risk assessment there were around 120 call centre telephone-based staff (Telephone Billing, dealing mainly with billing enquiries), and approximately 80 staff dealing with written enquiries and complaints (Post Billing). Each member of staff had a computer terminal that they used to access and update customer accounts and type letters. In Telephone Billing employees were split into teams of 10-15 people, all doing broadly similar work. Each team within Post Billing dealt with specific types of enquiries. Post Billing were allocated work as files in their 'in-trays'. Staff in Telephone Billing pressed a button on their telephone to indicate when they were ready to accept a call. Jobs in both sections involved a high degree of contact with staff in other parts of the organisation.

During Familiarisation, it was reported by employees and their managers that customer contact staff were struggling to meet rapidly increasing levels of customer demands. The Management Systems Audit revealed that in Telephone Billing only 25% of calls were being answered within 30 seconds, which was below the standard set by industry regulators. It appeared that targets set by industry regulators and senior management were extremely challenging given existing resources and work systems. The activity and performance of individuals in both sections were heavily monitored. Most parties agreed that, although there were staffing problems which required urgent action, changes to work systems would be required to keep pace with the anticipated increases in customer demands.

The project was initiated by the Health and Safety Department. There was concern about stress levels across the organisation. However, the organisation was keen to focus on Customer Contact Staff who were perceived as a 'high risk' group. Nevertheless, the day-to-day management of the project was carried out by a group set up locally at the customer contact site. A variety of people were involved in this Steering Group, including the project team, employees and management from both Telephone Billing and Post Billing, together with Health and Safety, Union, and welfare representatives.

3. PHASE I: RISK ASSESSMENT

3.1 PROCESS

The risk assessment involved identifying problems related largely to the design and management of work by gathering expert judgements about work from employees and management.

Workplace observations were extensive, and included sitting with staff while they carried out their work. The organisation also kept thorough records on performance, absence and turnover, which provided useful information throughout the project. Following Familiarisation, a series of 25 Work Analysis Interviews were carried out with a random selection of volunteers from both sections of the Customer Contact Centre. A further eight key stakeholders were involved in the Management Systems Audit. All this information was brought together in the design of the risk assessment survey. The Work Analysis Interviews and the comments of the Steering Group suggested that many stressors would be common to both groups of staff. Consequently just one version of the Work Environment Survey was used. The Steering Group helped to check the user-friendliness and coverage of the risk assessment questionnaire, and a number of useful and constructive changes were made.

The questionnaire was distributed in July 1997. At the request of management, staff were asked to complete the questionnaire outside of work time. 125 questionnaires were returned representing a response rate of 62%. Statistical analyses of the questionnaire data identified a number of likely risk factors. Information from the interviews, workplace observations and organisational documentation was used to illustrate and elaborate the questionnaire data.

3.2 RESULTS

3.2.1 Telephone Billing

In terms of their health profile, these employees reported being more 'worn out' (tired, confused, and emotional) than the national and industry averages. A fairly high percentage of them (59%) reported work-related musculoskeletal pain. Absence levels were relatively high (11 days per year), and relatively few were satisfied with their job (38%). Perhaps related to this, only 23% wished to remain in their present job. Information held by the organisation indicated that staff turnover was high. Staff reported many stressors. Many of these were challenges to employee well-being (risk factors). The likely risk factors and other major stressors appeared to be:

- Lack of time to finish jobs, coupled with a steady flow of demands to take on new jobs
- A lack of fairness in performance monitoring procedures
- Poor communication with other parts of the organisation, and a lack of information needed to assist customers with problems
- High workload and lack of line management support
- Lack of guidance about task ownership and unclear procedures for completing tasks
- Inadequate staffing and lack of breaks
- Too little emphasis on producing quality work – too much emphasis on quantity

This list of likely risk factors did not come as a surprise to the Steering Group, and was used as a starting point for discussions aimed at producing a package of interventions. As the risk assessment results were fed back to the organisation, plans were already underway to address some of the underlying causes of the stressors and risk factors.

3.2.2 Post Billing

The health profile of this group was similar in many ways to that of the Telephone Billing staff. Post Billing employees reported being more 'worn out' (tired, confused, and emotional) than the national average. On these measures their scores were similar to those of Telephone Billing staff. A large proportion of the group (54%) reported work-related musculoskeletal pain. Absence (7 days per year) and job satisfaction (53% satisfied with their job) were moderate. However, a relatively small proportion (28%) wished to remain in their present job. Company records indicated that although staff turnover in this group was relatively high, it was below the level recorded in Telephone Billing.

Analysis of the Work Environment Survey data identified a number of stressors. Some of these were risk factors that were linked to problems identified in the health profile of the group. A number of important stressors and likely risk factors associated with this health profile are listed below:

- High workload, including excessive re-work (putting right mistakes) and many repeat enquiries

- Too little emphasis on producing quality work with a heavy emphasis on quantity targets

- A lack of fairness in performance monitoring procedures

- Poor communication with other parts of the organisation, and lack of the information needed to assist customers with problems

- Inadequate staffing and poor line manager availability

- Lack of consultation by management

- Some slow IT systems

- Lack of guidance about the ownership of tasks

---

4. PHASE II: TRANSLATION AND RISK REDUCTION

The results from the risk assessment were communicated to the project Steering Group and the staff involved in September 1997. Three Steering Group meetings were held over the following weeks in order to design interventions to address the likely risk factors. During the intervention design phase, a new manager was appointed to oversee the running of the Telephone Billing section of customer services. This appointment had a major impact on the design and implementation of interventions. The new manager had devised - with some reference to the risk assessment results - a plan for developing and implementing new working methods that would improve performance. It also appeared that these 'interventions' would address some of the stressors and likely risk factors. Increased staffing levels had been secured to support this change process. Interventions suggested by the Steering Group were implemented within the framework of this change process.

A number of interventions implemented in Telephone Billing were produced by combining the results of the risk assessment with management consultations with staff and work done by 'Change Teams'. These were set up to devise innovative methods for improving efficiency in working practices and reducing the problems reported in the risk assessment. The introduction of the teams was part of the new manager's plan.

Having been informed of the plan to introduce the 'Change Teams' and support their suggestions, the Steering Group believed that this initiative could be an effective way of dealing with the underlying pathology (inefficient working methods) that was driving a number of risk factors and stressors. Initially, one of the work teams within Telephone Billing (around 15 staff and their Team Leader) was designated as a 'Change Team'. While they did their job, the team carried out a careful analysis of their work. From this analysis, the team devised and piloted ways of improving efficiency and standardising effective working methods. A high degree of employee participation was involved in making the 'Change Team' work. Ideas that were piloted successfully were gradually spread to the rest of the Telephone Billing section. More details of specific interventions devised by the teams are given in the Intervention Package section of this case study. Other interventions devised in this way dealt with other pathologies identified by the Steering Group (performance monitoring, staffing, inadequate formal communications with line management, lack of information, and long unbroken periods of work).

The interventions implemented in Post Billing were more directly driven by the Steering Group. As was the case with Telephone Billing, a number of changes occurred over the intervention period as a result of the natural development of the business and changes within other parts of the organisation. These were evaluated alongside the bespoke interventions. Steering Group discussions were structured in a way that produced a concrete action plan arising from a careful analysis of the underlying organisational pathology. This began with an identification of a number of driving factors, such as performance monitoring, time pressures, team leader staffing and organisational communication, that seemed to underlie a number of the issues raised during the risk assessment phase. This was an important step in making the problems appear manageable. The group then considered whether any of the problems would be tackled by changes that were already planned, such as the investment in new equipment or the Task Force (directed by senior managers) charged with improving organisational communication. The Task Force used information provided by local managers to identify the shortcomings in communication processes that directly affected the quality of service delivered to customers.

Actions which resulted from the initiative included the implementation of common sets of working practices, procedures and targets, and the reduction of local deviations from standard service delivery processes (through guidance to managers). These actions affected field operations staff (who worked closely with Customer Services staff) over the period of the intervention.

For those problems remaining, detailed action plans were developed by exploring a number of possible strategies. The practicalities of implementing these changes were then agreed. The intervention packages for the two sections of the Customer Contact Centre are outlined on the next two pages. For each organisational pathology, the intervention(s) targeted at addressing that problem are listed.

INTERVENTION PACKAGE 1
Telephone Billing

Organisational Pathology: Performance Monitoring

Introduction of a quality team. Staff trained to evaluate quality of calls on a number of criteria, with results fed back to staff by Team Leaders. Guidance was also given to staff on how to achieve standards. This intervention was driven by management rather than through the ideas of staff, and was designed to reduce the amount of re-work and improve the quality of service to customers. Each member of staff would be given training based on the results of the quality monitoring of their work.

Changes in performance targets, from calls per hour to amount of time working on calls and average call duration. This was part of the 'Change Team' package. The change was designed to allow flexibility in targets according to the type of call being dealt with. This was believed to be a fairer and less 'pressured' system.

Organisational Pathology: Ways of Working

Introduction of 'Change Team' guidance. This was a set of quick-reference manuals designed to help staff decide how different types of enquiries could be dealt with most efficiently and effectively. The guidance was piloted and documents produced by the Change Teams. It was hoped that staff would be able to deal with enquiries more quickly and with more confidence than before. It was also expected that the inclusion of specified contact points and referral routes for particular types of questions in the manuals would improve communication with other parts of the organisation.

Introduction of the 'Research' system: one member of staff in each team freed up from phone work to deal with longer and more complex enquiries, before phoning customers back. This was designed to free staff from calls which prevented them from keeping up with performance targets.

Organisational Pathology: Staffing and Work Organisation

Introduction of short fixed-time breaks: two official ten-minute breaks per day (in addition to a one hour lunch break, and opportunities to take brief 'unofficial' breaks) to allow staff more of a break from customer demands and screen work. Also, the hiring of new staff to help deal with growing demands.

Organisational Pathology: Information Systems

Easier and quicker access to information on IT systems, by 'tweaking' the system. This allowed staff an easier route to the information they needed, and it was hoped this would save time and frustration for them when they were dealing with customers. Also a training initiative ('Did You Know' sessions) to remind staff of the key points of important changes in procedures and policy affecting the way the job was done, and increased use of e-mail to notify staff of changes in policy and procedures. This intervention was designed to provide staff with the information they needed in order to assist customers effectively.

Organisational Pathology: Communications

Introduction of regular and structured team meetings to give staff the opportunity to raise problems, ask Team Leaders questions, and also to give management a forum to communicate important information.

Other Interventions

Re-grading of jobs via competency tests, to a level which reflected the demands of the job.

INTERVENTION PACKAGE 2
Post Billing

Organisational Pathology: Performance Monitoring

Introduction of a quality team. Staff were trained to evaluate quality of correspondence on a number of criteria, with results fed back to staff by Team Leaders. Based on the results of the quality monitoring, guidance and training were given to staff on how to achieve standards. Again, this intervention was driven by management to improve the service received by customers, while reducing the amount of re-work.

Consultation and negotiation about realistic targets for completion of various types of tasks. This intervention was designed to alleviate the pressure staff felt when they were working on long, or involved, jobs.

Organisational Pathology: Time Pressures

Introduction of a Customer Contact IT system, to manage the progress of enquiries and the way correspondence was dealt with (a time management and organisational aid). This was introduced in the complaints section only. The system reminded staff when tasks needed doing, and allowed them to see how far tasks had progressed. It was hoped the system would help staff to deal with multiple tasks and deadlines, and conflicting priorities.

Easier and quicker access to customer information held on IT systems, by 'tweaking' the system. This allowed staff to deal with correspondence more quickly.

Organisational Pathology: Staffing and Communications

An increase in the number of Team Leaders through the promotion of team members and secondments. Firming up of staffing by appointing long standing temporary staff to permanent posts. Additional Team Leaders were introduced to increase their availability to staff who needed to call upon them for advice.

The introduction of regular and structured team meetings to review quality and quantity of performance. Individual (one-to-one) meetings were also instigated. The main purpose of these interventions was to give staff a greater understanding of the need for performance monitoring. It was hoped that the intervention would help staff to see and use performance monitoring as an aid to skills development.

Organisational Pathology: Organisational Response

Faster responses from other parts of the organisation following the recommendations of, and changes made by, a cross-process Task Force. These interventions directly affected employees in other parts of the organisation. Knock-on effects were felt by Post Billing staff who dealt extensively with other parts of the organisation.

Other Interventions

The development of a 'skills matrix' to assist training and development, to sit alongside more frequent appraisals. These interventions were designed to equip staff with the skills needed to cope with all types of enquiries. The frequent appraisals were also designed to assist staff development and encourage the 'positive' use of performance statistics.

Investment in new office equipment and furniture to improve the comfort of workstations, workspace, and speed of access to information on IT systems. As a result of tougher monitoring of Display Screen Equipment usage, staff were encouraged to take more breaks.

5. PHASE III: EVALUATION

5.1 METHOD

Evaluation of the interventions was carried out using a number of methods. Initially, focus groups were used to explore the extent and possible impact of the interventions. Information from these helped to produce an intervention inventory. This allowed staff to indicate their awareness of, involvement in, and reactions to the interventions. Through discussions with the Steering Group it was decided that the evaluation questionnaire should focus on the key problem areas identified in the risk assessment. Self-reports of well-being, absence, and satisfaction were obtained again to help evaluate the impact of interventions. Organisational data on performance, absence, and turnover were also examined at this time and compared to those gathered during the original risk assessment survey.

The evaluation questionnaire was distributed by Team Leaders in November 1998. As with the risk assessment survey, this was checked and agreed with the project steering group. Unlike the risk assessment survey, staff were allowed to complete the questionnaire during work time. 115 questionnaires were returned, a response rate of 47%. In terms of their average age and length of service, those completing the assessment were similar to those who completed the original risk assessment.

5.2 RESULTS

5.2.1 Telephone Billing

Differences Between 1997 and 1998

Analysis of the evaluation questionnaire revealed a number of changes in relation to the likely risk factors and stressors. Compared to the results from the 1997 survey, many more staff were positive about the amount of feedback they received about the quality of their work and the way their manager monitored the quality of their work (see Figure 1). A much lower proportion (48%) reported that performance statistics did not reflect the amount of effort they put in (compared to 79% in 1997). A larger proportion reported that quality work was adequately recognised. Recognition of effort appeared to have improved (47% rating it as a problem compared with 74% in 1997). Lack of management guidance was still a problem for 63% of staff, but this compared positively with 86% in 1997.

In 1997, virtually all staff had said that inadequate breaks were provided. In 1998, less than half reported that this was still a problem (see Figure 1). Significantly fewer staff reported that they were allowed inadequate time away from their desk if they were upset by a customer (40% reporting it as a problem in 1998, compared with 65% in 1997).

Problems involving line management also showed significant signs of improvement. The proportion of staff reporting that availability and communication were problems had halved (see Figure 1). The proportion reporting that the level of support they received from their line manager was a problem dropped from 47% to 26%. Action taken by management after consultation had also improved (55% rating it as a problem compared to 84% in 1997).

Figure 1 shows that large changes were observed for problems with organisational communication. Quality of information (82% reporting the problem in 1997 compared with 45% in 1998), and help (78% reporting the problem in 1997 compared with 39% in 1998), from field operatives (and other sections of the organisation) showed marked improvement. More staff reported being adequately informed about work affecting customer supplies. There was also an improvement in communication with senior management (31% fewer rating it as a problem), but this remained a problem reported by 63% of staff.

In 1997, almost every member of staff reported that staffing levels and long unbroken periods of screen work were problems. In 1998, less than one in five reported that staffing was a problem, with only half reporting that unbroken periods of screen work was still a problem (see Figure 1). Far fewer staff reported that they were dealing with large numbers of complex enquiries (42% compared with 65% in 1997), and the number of staff reporting re-work as a problem had also dropped markedly (from 92% reporting the problem, to 62%). The proportion who believed their pay was unfair had also halved (from 53% to 29%).

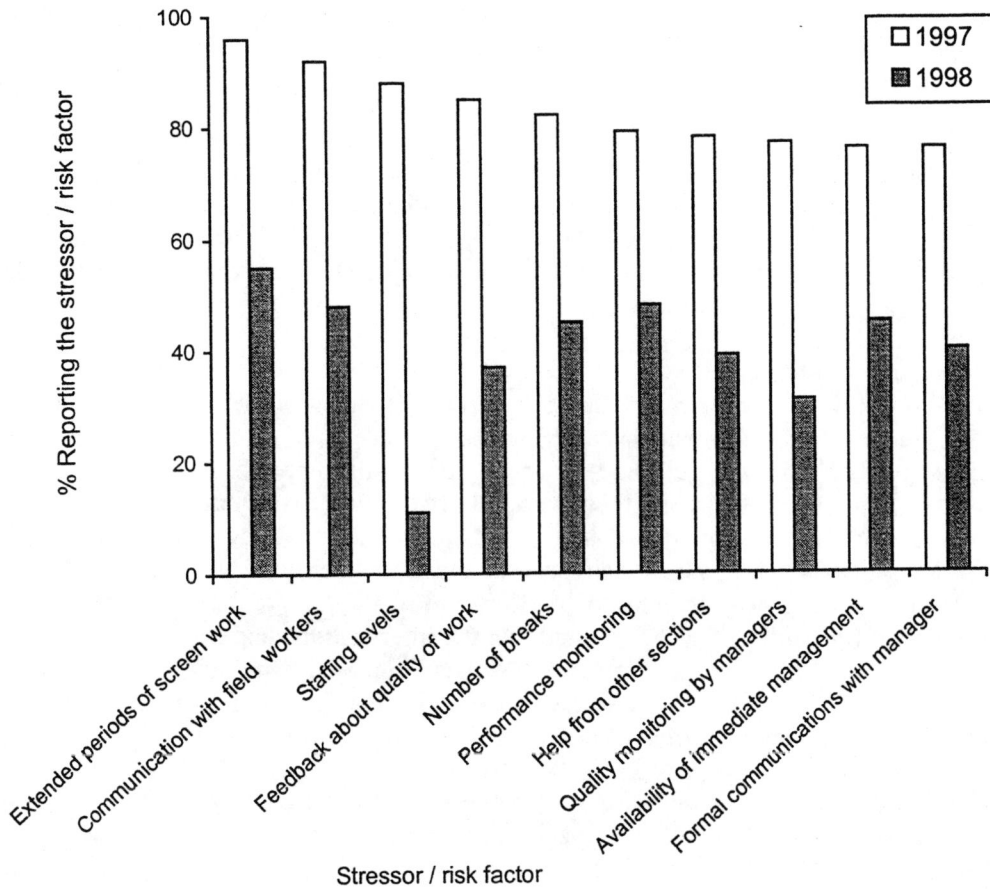

Figure 1: Changes in job design and management (1997 – 1998) 10 major improvements

Changes in the performance of the section were impressive. 95% of calls were answered in less than 30 seconds in July 1998, compared with only 25% in the same month of 1997. Only 2% of customers were abandoning their calls, compared with 12% the year before, even though call volume had actually increased over the year.

As a direct result of some of the interventions, call waiting times were reduced substantially and managers reported that fewer customers were irate as a result of waiting for long periods. Such changes had implications for working conditions. In the evaluation survey, employees were asked whether these changes had improved their work. Three quarters of the staff reported that the hiring of new staff had improved their work. 60% noted that fewer customers were angry at waiting times – nearly all said that this had made their working conditions better. Around half of the staff (50% and 59% respectively) reported that increases in the amount of time between calls and reductions in the number of calls abandoned (customers hanging-up) had improved their work.

Interestingly, the overall health profile remained very similar to that obtained in 1997. Organisational data revealed that absence was reduced and now remained steady at around 5%. This was judged as acceptable by the organisation. There was little overall change on measures of job satisfaction, intention to leave, or reports of musculoskeletal pain. 'Worn out' and 'tense' scores were steady.

Organisational Penetration and Impact of the Interventions

Dramatic changes in judgements about aspects of work were accompanied by a high level of awareness of the interventions. At least 70% of staff were aware of all but one of the interventions (changes in the IT system). For most of the changes staff reported being either directly involved in, or significantly affected by, the change. Where staff were not actively involved, the interventions had involved the relaying of information, for example through the re-launch of the company's mission statement. Knowledge of such 'passive' interventions is the best that can be expected. Most staff knew about such changes. With the exception of certain aspects of quality monitoring and the use of e-mail to convey important information, few staff reacted negatively to the interventions.

Performance Monitoring

Half of those involved in training resulting from quality monitoring and half of those aware of quality guidance indicated that these changes had made their work better. Those staff who indicated that training and guidance resulting from quality monitoring and reductions in the amount of re-work had improved their work reported lower 'worn out' scores and made more positive evaluations of support and help from line managers. They were also more likely to report job satisfaction. Positive responses to these interventions were also linked to more favourable evaluations of recognition of effort and quality, appreciation from customers, and line manager availability. Those who said that the interventions had improved their work were less likely to want to leave the company. Most staff reported being affected by a reduction in the amount of re-work. Three quarters of those indicated that the reduction in the amount of mistakes that they had to put right (re-work) had improved their job.

It appeared that the introduction of quality monitoring, which was in its early stages at the time of the evaluation, had placed extra demands on all staff. Two-thirds reported that monitoring of the quality of their work, and the resultant feedback on their performance, had made their job worse. Unfortunately, but unsurprisingly, those staff who reported that the introduction of quality monitoring had made their work worse also reported high 'worn out' scores. Interestingly, however, most of the those who had been involved in training resulting from quality monitoring indicated that their job had improved as a result. Further, compared to the risk assessment results, staff reported that the recognition of quality work had improved. In this sense the quality monitoring appeared to be a double-edged sword. Information gathered during the focus group sessions indicated that staff were uncertain about the quality standards required. There also appeared to be a perception that the 'marking' of quality was inconsistent.

Changes in performance targets were well received by around one in three. Many reported that the intervention made no difference to their work. Those who reported that changes in performance targets had made their work better were less likely to report musculoskeletal pain and more likely to report being satisfied with their job overall. They were also more likely to make positive evaluations of line manager communication, help and support.

Ways of Working

63% of those affected by the introduction of the in-team 'Research' scheme reported that it had improved their work. Staff who indicated that the 'Research' scheme had improved their work reported lower 'worn out' scores. In terms of job design, they also indicated that the allocation of work was fair and were less likely to want to leave the company. Half of those who were aware of 'Change' guidance on how calls should be dealt with and which ones should be 'Research' calls indicated that the information had improved their work. Those who stated that 'Change' guidance had improved their job reported lower 'worn out' scores. They also made more positive evaluations of appreciation from customers, the level of teamwork, and were more likely to be satisfied with their job.

Work Organisation

The fixed-time breaks were only set up three weeks before the evaluation, and it was unlikely that their impact could be evaluated with any certainty with data gathered at the time of the evaluation. The large number of staff who reported that the hiring of new staff (and the resultant changes in customer demands) had made their job better were more likely to report that line manager help and support were good, complex enquiries were less of a problem, and demands from line management were acceptable. They were also more likely to report that opportunities for taking breaks were adequate.

Information Systems

'Did You Know' sessions had affected nearly all staff, and 85% of them indicated their work had improved as a result. It was not possible to evaluate the effects of the 'Did You Know' sessions since virtually all staff evaluated them positively. This in itself represents a favourable evaluation. Despite a mixed reception, those staff who reacted positively to the increased use of e-mail to announce changes in policies and procedures tended to report lower 'worn out' scores than those staff (the majority) who reacted negatively. The small number of staff who reported that quicker access to information on IT systems had improved their work were more likely to report that the effort they put in and the quality of their work was adequately recognised. They were more likely to report that communication with senior management and management action after employee consultation were adequate.

Communications

The majority of staff had been involved in the introduction of regular team meetings, and 62% of them saw those meetings as a positive step. At the time of the evaluation a large proportion of the staff had started to take fixed-time breaks, with 67% indicating that these had improved their work. Staff who reported that the introduction of regular and structured team meetings had improved their work were more likely to report that appreciation from customers, support from work about home problems, and support and help from line management were adequate. These staff were more likely to report being satisfied with their job overall, and less likely to report work-related musculoskeletal pain.

Other Problem Areas

Most staff had been affected by the pay related intervention of re-grading through competency tests. This was well received by 56% of those involved, a figure that may have reflected an unsuccessful outcome for some employees. The majority of staff agreed that the re-grading of jobs had been a positive step. These staff reported lower 'worn out' scores, and were less likely to report high absence. Unsurprisingly, these staff were the most likely to report that their pay was fair. They were also more likely to report adequate opportunities to use the skills learned in training. Overall, they were also more likely to be satisfied with their work. 60% of staff reported that a loyalty bonus they had received had improved their job.

5.2.2 Post Billing

Differences Between 1997 and 1998

For these employees, changes tended to be less dramatic than those reported in Telephone Billing. For example, although fewer staff reported problems with the way the quality of work was recognised and monitored, the changes were smaller than in the Telephone Billing section.

However, there was a large drop in the proportion of staff who reported that they were not given enough time to see enquiries through to a conclusion. In 1997, 61% of staff reported that this aspect of their work was a problem. The figure was only 38% in 1998. Similarly, lack of breaks was a problem for 52% of staff in 1997, with the figure dropping to 22% in 1998. In 1997 three-quarters of staff reported that unrealistic goals were set for customer service; this figure was 45% in 1998.

In the 1997 survey, three-fifths of staff reported that communication with field operatives and the quality of information received from them were problems. In 1998 only around one in five reported these aspects of work to be problems (see Figure 2). There was a smaller drop in the percentage of staff reporting problems with communication with other parts of the organisation, from 85% in 1997 to 59% in 1998.

Fewer staff reported problems with getting help from other sections of the organisation (dropping from 63% to 46%). A smaller proportion of staff indicated that lack of guidance about the ownership of problems was a difficulty (down to 52% from 72%). A drop of almost 40% (from 63% in 1997 to 24% in 1998) was observed in the proportion of staff reporting that lack of information about major works was a problem.

In the 1998 survey less than 20% of staff reported that their workstation was inadequate, while in 1997 this figure was close to 60%. The percentage of staff rating office space as a problem had fallen by a similar amount (see Figure 2). There was also a drop in the number of staff reporting problems with long periods of screen work and poor work equipment (see Figure 2). However, two aspects of work were judged to be a problem by a greater proportion of staff in 1998 than they were in 1997. These were staffing levels and overall level of pay.

% Reporting the stressor / risk factor

100

80

60

40

20

0

1997
1998

Information on progress of work
Unrealistic targets
Unbroken screen work / poor equipment
Communications with field workers
Information about major work
Time to finish jobs
Quality of information from the field
Office space
Workstation
Break taking arrangements

Stressor / risk factor

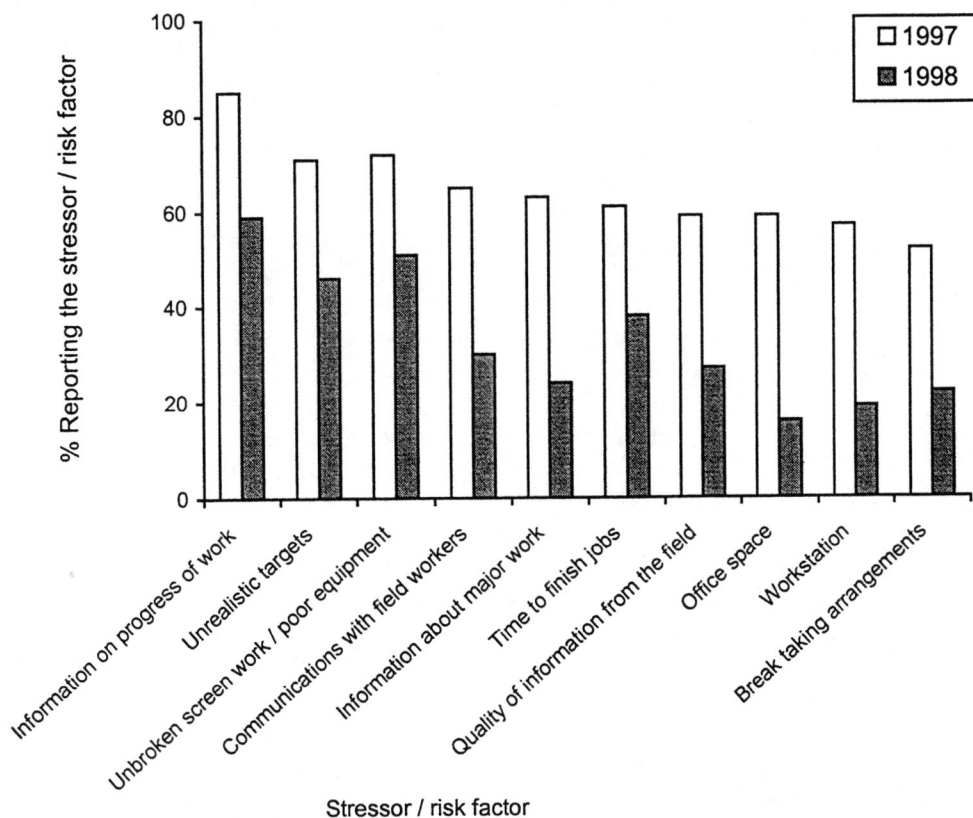

Figure 2: Changes in job design and management (1997 – 1998) 10 major improvements

Overall, the health profile remained steady, but with some improvements. Staff reported being more 'worn out' than average, and there was little change on measures of job satisfaction, intention to leave the company, or musculoskeletal pain. However, month-to-month comparisons using organisational data showed absence down from 8% to 4%.

Organisational Penetration and Impact of the Interventions

These modest but important changes were anticipated since some of the interventions were only applicable or important to certain jobs in the section. A variety of different roles existed within the Post Billing section, with some interventions only affecting people in certain roles. For example, the introduction of the 'Customer Contact System' only impacted upon those staff dealing with complaints. Information gathered during the focus group sessions indicated that there had been some significant changes in working conditions over the year or so since the risk assessment. The results of the evaluation survey supported these findings.

In addition to the bespoke interventions, there was a change in personnel at senior management within the organisation. This resulted in the opening up of new lines of communication (including direct e-mail access to directorate level), and a re-launch of the company's mission statement. At the evaluation stage, staff in both sections were asked about the impact of these changes. Most staff were aware of the re-launch of the company's mission statement and the appointment of new directors. Most reported these had not made any difference to their work. However, of those who were aware of the availability of direct lines of communication with senior management, half said it had improved their work. These staff were less likely to want to leave the company. They were also more positive about the amount of guidance about the ownership of work and the adequacy of communication with field based workers.

Performance Monitoring

Around half of the staff had been involved in quality monitoring and received feedback from those sessions. Few staff reported that the interventions had made their work worse. This was a much more positive response than that observed in Telephone Billing. Staff who indicated that quality monitoring, feedback, and guidance had improved their job were less likely to report problems with demands to take on new tasks before they had finished jobs in progress. These staff were also more likely to report that performance targets were realistic and achievable, teamwork was good, and that the level of demands from management was acceptable.

Time Pressures

Most staff were aware that Team Leaders had been consulting staff about realistic times for completing work, with 60% reporting that their work had improved as a result. When consultation and negotiation about realistic targets were recognised, staff generally indicated that they had improved working conditions. Staff making such positive evaluations were more likely to indicate that the amount of feedback about the quality of work was adequate. They were also more likely to report that line managers were available, supportive, and helpful and that communication with them was adequate.

Only around a third of staff had been affected by the introduction of the Customer Contact System. This was to be expected because the system had only been introduced for those staff dealing with complaints, due to a lack of resources. Almost all of those who were using the new system said that its introduction had improved their work. Those who said Customer Contact had made a difference to their job were more likely to report that performance targets were realistic and achievable. The system also seemed to have impacted upon communications. Staff reacting positively to the change were more likely to indicate that communication with, and quality of information received from, field operations was adequate. These staff were also more likely to report being satisfied with their job overall. Changes to the IT system were enthusiastically endorsed, with too few staff indicating that the changes made 'no difference' to their work for comparisons to be made.

Staffing & Communications

Most staff reported that they had been directly involved in more regular team meetings about statistical performance monitoring, and half of those involved reported that their work was improved by them. These staff reported lower 'worn out' scores. They were also more likely to indicate that performance statistics reflected the amount of effort put in, that effort was adequately recognised, and that task allocation was fair. The intervention was clearly linked to the actions of line management. Staff evaluating the intervention positively were more likely to report that line manager help and support were adequate, and less likely to report problems with demands to take on new or urgent jobs while others were in progress. Staff were generally aware of an increase in Team Leaders, but less than half of those said their work was better as a result. Few staff (around a quarter) reported that increased Team Leader availability had affected them. However, nearly all of these staff reported that their work had improved as a result. Staff who indicated that an increase in the number of Team Leaders had improved their work reported lower 'worn out' scores and made more positive evaluations of the recognition of quality work. Unsurprisingly, they were also more likely to report that line manager availability was adequate.

Organisational Response

60% had noticed quicker response times from staff in other parts of the organisation, with over half reporting this improvement had made their work better. These staff were more likely to be positive about the guidance offered about the ownership of problems. As would be expected, they also made more positive evaluations of communications with field based workers.

Other Problem Areas

Around half of the staff reported being affected by increased frequency of appraisals, though most said their work was no different as a result. Most staff knew about the introduction of return to work interviews, but few had direct experience of them. A similar picture emerged for the skills matrix, with only a handful of staff reporting that it had had a positive impact on their work. Nearly all of the staff had noticed, or been affected by, changes in office layout and equipment. These changes were positively received by the vast majority, with 75% reporting that their job had improved as a result. A large proportion of staff (60%) had been affected by the changes in the IT system. Again, most of those staff (85%) indicated that their work had improved as a result. However, no specific effects were identified for these interventions. The effects of appraisals and new training programmes may only be evident when they have been in place for longer than a year. Investment in new office equipment and furniture and the changes to the IT system were enthusiastically endorsed: statistical evaluation of their impact was not possible since too few staff indicated that the intervention had made no difference. However, these findings, in themselves, indicated that the interventions were positive steps.

Commentary: Telephone Billing and Post Billing Interventions

Given the initial problems identified in the risk assessment and the demanding nature of the work being carried out by the customer contact staff, these results were received as encouraging. However, bearing in mind the rapidly changing nature of work in the Customer Contact Centre, it was recommended that stressors remaining at the evaluation stage be monitored and further attempts made to tackle them.

6. LEARNING POINTS

6.1 DECISION MAKING

The project was initiated within the central management structure of the company by the Health and Safety Department, but the management of the project was taken on by a locally based Steering Group. Local management of the project, with central management backing, facilitated quicker decision making and smoothed the logistics of the project. Across all the case studies, the quickest progress was made in projects managed 'close' to the risk assessment group, with full senior management support 'backing up'.

6.2 THE STEERING GROUP

Both local management backing and full employee involvement were essential. Experienced and trusted staff from both parties were included in the Steering Group. Time was taken at the beginning of the project to set realistic expectations among those involved in the Steering Group. Preparing the Steering Group in this way helped the project team gather the necessary organisational expertise as the project progressed. As a result, no meetings were held up by repeated questions and explanations about aims and objectives.

6.3 ENTHUSIASM

The main challenge facing this project was generating enthusiasm within a group faced with a heavy workload. Relatively small groups of staff were involved and high response rates were crucial. Posters appeared on noticeboards, in staff canteens and even on the doors of staff toilets. An article appeared in the company newspaper, and e-mails were sent to staff which gave detailed information about the project. The project was publicised using all available media. The Steering Group provided valuable information about effective media. Clear and positive language should be used in publicity material. Results should be communicated to staff at key stages of the project.

6.4 RESPONSE RATES

The questionnaire used was detailed. Staff were not allowed time to complete the risk assessment questionnaire at work. In order to manage problems with the response rate, the Steering Group was mobilised and asked to chase up responses in each area. The project team also spent two days on site encouraging people to fill out questionnaires, answering questions and addressing the concerns of staff. The sudden flood of questionnaires this effort brought about was testimony to its effectiveness. Adding these 'personal touches' is preferable to just delivering a 'faceless' questionnaire.

6.5 CHANGING PERSONNEL

Over the course of the project, the staff involved in driving it forward may change. At the intervention design phase the involvement of the newly appointed Call Centre Manager was crucial. The risk assessment was explained to him, and the usefulness of the results in planning changes for Telephone Billing was pointed out. He responded enthusiastically and tailored some of his ideas and plans to address the key concerns that staff raised in the risk assessment.

Being able to combine the results of the risk assessment with planned change is crucial to the implementation, and success, of the interventions. As the composition of a Steering Group changes, time should be taken to explain the project to new members. The appointment of new personnel in key positions can be an opportunity to add impetus to the change process.

6.6 INTERVENTION DESIGN: END-USER INPUT

The most positive part of the intervention design phase was the enthusiastic input of staff into the process. The methods for change instigated by the Telephone Billing Manager (e.g. the 'Change' team) allowed staff to formulate solutions to a number of problems. Directed effort by staff, with management support, was the key to the design of a package of interventions which was generally well received by staff.

6.7 ORGANISATIONAL TURBULENCE

Change over any sustained project period is inevitable. When planning the evaluation stage, senior managers raised the possibility that the physical layout of the offices might be altered. It was anticipated that this would be a difficult period for staff. The decision was made to carry out the evaluation in a period of relative stability and this may have contributed to some encouraging findings. As long as project momentum is not lost, short delays can be used to avoid times when staff are placed under unusually heavy demands or when there is a period of uncertainty. When a turbulent backdrop cannot be avoided, or when the impact of radical change is of interest, survey results should be interpreted carefully taking into account the context of the change.

6.8 INTERVENTION INVENTORIES

Both managers and staff were questioned in order to catalogue the 'real' interventions. Management tended to focus on carefully planned and managed high profile changes, while staff focused on the more immediate aspects of their work – for example, the 'Did You Know' sessions. A list of all the changes that may have affected employees (an intervention inventory) needs to be gathered before the evaluation phase. As businesses develop and grow, changes occur that impact upon working conditions. Therefore, it would have been uninformative only to measure the impact of interventions emanating directly from the risk assessment. One or two interventions were not well received by staff. The detailed questions included in the evaluation questionnaire identified the 'pros and cons' of these interventions. Both management and staff viewed quality monitoring as vital to the improvement of the service offered to customers. The 1998 evaluation survey provided information on how it could be best utilised to the satisfaction of staff.

6.9 CONTINUOUS IMPROVEMENT

The evaluation phase should not be the end of any project, but rather a starting point for continuous improvement. The results of the evaluation phase received a positive response from the project Steering Group. Inevitably problems remained. Telephone Billing staff still identified performance targets, control over their work, time pressures, training and slow computer systems as problems. Staff in Post Billing reported problems with recognition of effort and quality, line manager availability, staffing, job insecurity and training. While emphasising the positive findings from the project, the need for further work in some areas has been identified and acknowledged. Narrower and more focused assessments can be used to keep track of persistent problems. Between assessments, systems should be in place to help management 'keep an eye' on the problems.

CASE STUDY 2

RETAIL STAFF

1. SUMMARY

The study was carried out among two groups of employees from a large retail organisation in the south of England: Customer Services staff and Night / Evening Shift staff.

1.1 PHASE I: RISK ASSESSMENT

The risk assessment was carried out in September 1997, using versions of the Work Environment Survey tailored to the needs and contexts of the two groups of employees. The risk assessment survey identified different profiles of likely risk factors for the two groups of staff.

Customer Services Staff

In comparison to similar work groups, Customer Services staff reported a relatively good health profile, except for high levels of musculoskeletal disorders. However, a number of stressors relating to the design and management of their work were reported. These included issues to do with time pressures, performance monitoring, lack of support and lack of appreciation by management, and lack of training. Some of these proved to be likely risk factors in terms of some of the health problems reported by the group.

Night / Evening Shift Staff

The health profile of this group contrasted sharply with that of the Customer Services Staff. A relatively large proportion of staff reported poor well-being, musculoskeletal disorders, lack of sleep, job dissatisfaction, intention to leave the company and recent involvement in a workplace accident.

A number of stressors and likely risk factors (problems associated with problems in the health profile) were targeted for intervention. These included time pressures; unfair pay; poor communication with management; high demands from management, colleagues and cover staff; poor quality equipment; lack of support from Store Managers; absence amongst colleagues; lack of flexibility in hours; lack of communication about new procedures; and intimidation at work.

1.2 PHASE II: TRANSLATION AND RISK REDUCTION

The results from the risk assessment were used to design specific interventions and shape on-going and planned future changes. Through Steering Group meetings and employee consultation, a plan of action was agreed in August 1998. Many of the interventions were cross-cutting changes that were designed to impact upon more than one group of employees and on the underlying pathology of a cluster of the likely risk factors and stressors described above. A broad package of interventions included staff and management meetings; open surgeries with Store Managers; store newsletters; overlapping shifts; increased access to e-mail; information on methods of best practice; harassment awareness and management training; 'return to work' interviews for absentees; swap sheets for shift staff; flexi-hours for supervisors; separate customer services desks managed by an experienced member of staff; improvements in store equipment; and changes in customer complaints policies.

1.3 PHASE III: EVALUATION

The evaluation was carried out in December 1998. Inevitably, some stressors remained. However, the evaluation revealed:

- Reasonable levels of awareness of, and involvement in, the interventions
- Positive reactions to a number of the interventions
- Improvements in employees' perceptions of the adequacy of their working conditions
- Employees involved in some interventions tended to report the most positive well-being

Bearing in mind that the interventions were only in place for a short period of time, these results were received as encouraging. Although further work needed to be done to address stressors within the organisation, significant progress was made during the case study.

2. BACKGROUND

The organisation involved in this case study commands a major share of the retail sector. The company has grown considerably over the last twenty years, opening a number of new and larger stores. This expansion has brought with it a number of changes in working practices. Recent changes included a move away from management hierarchies and status-based benefits to a much flatter management structure, introduction of performance management appraisals and a programme for change management for senior managers.

Contact with the organisation was made through the company's Occupational Health Manager. The organisation was examining various methods to deal with work related stress, and was keen to invest in a pro-active approach to tackling the sources of stress. To keep the project to a manageable size it was decided that a number of large stores within a particular region should be included in the case study. Six stores from the London and South-West England region were chosen. Because a large number of different jobs existed within each store, it was also decided that two groups of staff should be included in the project: the higher-graded staff within Customer Services, and staff on the Night and Evening Shift.

Around 80 Customer Services staff were involved in two main activities: providing operational support to checkout staff (cashing up, checking customer pricing queries, dealing with checkout problems) and dealing directly with enquiries from customers (e.g. the return of products, questions about services such as reward card schemes, etc.). Their other tasks involved dealing with shoplifters, answering the telephone, or working as a cashier at kiosks. Their jobs were extremely varied and hectic.

Night and Evening shift staff were involved in the replenishment of goods, usually after the store had closed. Around 160 took part in the project. Much of their job involved moving goods from storage areas onto trolleys, and then into the shopping area of the store. They had to deal with stock management information from computerised systems, and many supervised other staff. Even for senior grades the job could be very 'hands-on', with all staff being under pressure to re-stock the store before it re-opened in the morning. In some of the busier stores this could be an extremely challenging target. As the project began, the job was in the process of being re-organised to make teams of staff responsible for dealing with particular areas within the stores.

Because of the involvement of two groups of staff, the Steering Group was large. Employees from both groups were represented. Store Managers from the stores involved also took part in these meetings. In order to maintain support and momentum for the project, the group also included senior and middle management, and representatives from Occupational Health and Personnel.

3. PHASE I : RISK ASSESSMENT

3.1 PROCESS

Familiarisation involved workplace observation and interviews in all six stores. Organisational records and documentation (e.g. absence summaries, job descriptions, staff turnover, etc.) were also examined at both Head Office and the stores involved in the project. 30 Work Analysis Interviews were carried out and involved staff from each group in each store. Management Systems Audit Interviews were conducted with employees at regional and national Head Offices. These various sources of information indicated that the work carried out, and problems faced, by the two groups of employees were very different. Consequently, two versions of the Work Environment Survey were used in the risk assessment survey. The Steering Group provided a valuable input into the design process.

The complete survey instrument was distributed by each store's personnel managers within each of the selected stores in October 1997. Employees were given a specific time slot in which they were asked to attend a meeting, away from their work setting, during which they completed the risk assessment survey. The personnel managers were present at these meetings to answer the questions or concerns of staff. Staff were asked to return their completed survey in a sealed envelope either directly to the project team or via a collection box in each store. A reasonable overall response rate was achieved (43% for Customer Services Staff and 42% for Night / Evening Shift staff).

3.2 RESULTS

3.2.1 Customer Services Staff

The health profile of Customer Services Staff revealed a number of positive results. Compared with similar groups of staff from other organisations, Customer Services staff reported equivalent levels of feeling 'worn out' but indicated feeling less 'tense'. Job satisfaction, the proportion of staff wanting to leave and the pattern of health related behaviour were in line with national averages. Sickness absence appeared to be low (4 days per year). One problematical finding was a high incidence of musculoskeletal pain (60% reporting work-related pain).

Although the profile was generally good, it was possible to identify a number of likely risk factors from expert judgements about working conditions. The assessment identified the following likely risk factors and stressors:

- Poor performance monitoring, lack of quality feedback from management, lack of ongoing training

- Excessive demands from managers, lack of support from managers when dealing with customers, lack of appreciation from management and the Company

- Too little time for record keeping and stock replenishment, covering the work of others, working alone for long spells, excessive demands to take on extra work, demands to do two jobs at once

- Lack of rest breaks, lack of staff during busy periods

- Customers' lack of understanding of Customer Services' role, cramped conditions and poor equipment availability

3.2.2 Night / Evening Shift Staff

The health profile of this group of employees indicated a number of problem areas. These staff reported being more 'worn out' than comparable groups of shift-workers or manual workers. Most (69%) were not satisfied with their job. A large proportion (71%) indicated they were experiencing work-related musculoskeletal pain. Some also reported being recently involved in a workplace accident (generally slips, trips or falls).

Statistical analyses of questionnaire data revealed a number of stressors and aspects of work that were linked to problems with the health profile, i.e. likely risk factors:

- Difficult and poorly defined tasks (with too many changes in procedures and unclear goals)

- Lack of communication with immediate manager, lack of communication about new procedures, lack of support from store manager, lack of support from work about home problems, inflexible hours

- Problems with performance management (perception of unfair targets, lack of good quality feedback, lack of training)

- Excessive demands from colleagues, cover staff, and day shift management

- Time pressures and a lack of variability in workload

- Absence amongst colleagues, working with inexperienced staff, and problems with quality of work done by cover staff

- Lack of consultation in choice of equipment, and inadequate participation in decisions

- Intimidation at work

- Poor environmental conditions and store equipment

4. PHASE II : TRANSLATION AND RISK REDUCTION

The results from the risk assessment were fed back to the Steering Group in October 1997. There were a few surprises, but the Steering Group agreed that the risk assessment had managed to isolate the important stressors and the likely risk factors. A series of Steering Group meetings were then held between January and August 1998, in order to consider the design and implementation of interventions. Employees from both groups were heavily involved in this process, as were the managers of the stores taking part.

The intervention design process drew heavily on the framework for translation outlined in Part I of the Report, designed to identify the organisational pathology underlying the various symptoms, or likely risk factors and stressors, and used a number of the associated aids to planning (Section 5.2.2 of Part I of the Report). After feedback of the assessment results, the Steering Group split forces into 'Task Groups' to consider interventions, based on the results of the risk assessment, separately for each group of staff. These indicated that different risk factors and hazards existed for the two groups. However, the whole Steering Group reconvened at key stages to discuss progress.

The Task Groups were facilitated by the project team and informed experts from within the organisation (e.g. the Occupational Health Manager). Underlying issues (pathologies) were quickly identified. For Customers Services staff these were: inadequate communication and support structures for problem solving with management, the visible and varied role of staff limiting the amount of time available to complete tasks, and problems with the physical working environment associated with the location of Customer Services desks and the equipment provided in them. For Night / Evening Shift staff, a cluster of issues associated with inadequate communication and support structures for problem solving with management was also identified. Other underlying issues identified were: inadequate co-operation between day and night shift management, problems with absence management, a lack of flexibility in shiftwork hours, and under-investment in store equipment.

Once this 'clustering' had been achieved, a number of aids to planning were used to design interventions. While facilitation was designed to help the groups produce reasonably practicable solutions, some freedom was given to foster a creative and innovative atmosphere. However, the need to consider the logistics for implementing the changes was also stressed. The sessions were lively and produced a number of original ideas.

After the final session, intervention packages were drawn up which were supported by detailed implementation plans. These outlined details such as responsibilities, key players and timescales. For example, the Store Newsletter was to be the responsibility of Store Managers, and would be produced monthly, by staff.

Inevitably, some checks needed to be made regarding the practicality of the suggested interventions. This was achieved by consulting senior and Store Managers. Very few objections or problems were raised. One or two changes proved similar to those being planned or implemented by the organisation, and these were removed to avoid duplication. Generally the interventions were considered reasonable and sensible. Consultation with senior management was also used as an opportunity to gather information about changes which were due to take place over the intervention period. The results of these consultations were relayed to the Steering Group.

A final plan of action was drawn up in July 1998, by which time action had already begun on some of the interventions. Summaries of the interventions for each of the two groups of employees are presented on the following pages, together with the targeted problems.

INTERVENTION PACKAGE 1
Customer Services Staff

Organisational Pathology: Communication and Problem Solving

Staff meetings for Customer Services staff with their department manager were implemented on a weekly basis. These meetings were designed to address a number of workload and communication issues. The Task Group believed that many problems persisted because of the lack of a regular forum to discuss work problems and solutions. It was thought that this intervention would lead to changes over time that would improve the job at store level.

An Open Surgery when the store manager was available to staff. Initially, this was for half an hour each week. Again this was seen as a way of opening up lines of communication. Customer Services staff often worked with Store Managers when dealing with certain types of complaints, but had little time to discuss ideas for improving work.

Monthly meetings for all levels of store management were instigated. Staff reported that excessive demands often arose from other parts of the store. For example, demands to cover the work of others, or comments about housekeeping issues from managers in other sections. The Customer Services Task Group believed this problem could be addressed by improving understanding of the work done, and problems faced, by Customer Services.

A Store Newsletter was set up in the stores involved to inform staff of developments within the store and the company. The newsletter was produced in each store and included work-related and social information. The newsletter provided management with a way of passing on good news and positive feedback to a large number of employees in a document they would be likely to read.

Organisational Pathology: Time Pressures and the Visible Role

Time management courses for Customer Services staff were introduced. As part of a training programme introduced across the organisation, a number of Customer Services staff were due to attend the session. If effective, it was thought this would help staff to manage hectic workloads.

Separate Customer Services desks were not present in some stores, meaning that employees dealt with records or paperwork behind a desk which was also used for customer enquiries. This resulted in cramped working conditions and frequent interruptions. Separate Customer Services desks were constructed, and staffed by experience employees. This separated many customer enquiries from administrative work. It was recommended that capital earmarked for investment in equipment be targeted at new checkout chairs. Some Customer Services staff spent significant amounts of time covering checkout work.

Organisational Pathology: Work Equipment

More equipment was made available at the Customer Services desk. In dealing with paperwork, a number of pieces of stationery were required. This intervention was simply to increase the availability and quality of such materials by, for example, putting a 'bank style' pen on the Customer Services desk.

INTERVENTION PACKAGE 1 (continued)
Customer Services Staff

Other Issues

A 'Buddy System' was introduced for new Customer Services supervisors. They were allocated a more experienced member of staff as their *buddy* to help them through the early problems of managing their workload and supervising staff.

Changes in the customer complaints policy were introduced at some stores to allow staff to deal with complaints related to costs of up the value of £10.00. This was aimed at reducing the number of instances in which management approval was needed for decisions.

An organisation-wide training initiative was implemented to help managers become aware of behaviours which could make staff feel harassed or intimidated. Although not designed by the Steering Group, this intervention was thought to be directly relevant to problems related to demands from management.

INTERVENTION PACKAGE 2
Night / Evening Shift Staff

Organisational Pathology: Communication & Problem Solving

Introduction of open surgery: Store Managers to be available to see staff for half an hour per week. This was a cross-cutting intervention in that it was designed by the team working on interventions for Customers Services staff. However, poor communication was a particularly salient issue in the risk assessment for this group, and many Store Managers arranged to either work occasional night shifts, or surgery hours appropriate for this group.

The introduction of a monthly management meeting for all levels of store management. A number of the likely risk factors identified for this group (e.g. lack of consultation and communication and excessive demands) were driven by isolation from others in the store. These meetings were designed to increase understanding of the problems faced by the Night Shift, and to give them opportunities to participate in decisions that affected their job.

The Store Newsletter intervention was believed to be an improvement that would have a particular impact on the Night Shift, because of their lack of direct contact with the majority of store staff.

News about changes and developments within the company was often relayed over an e-mail system. Access to e-mail was introduced for night shift managers to enable them to pass this information on to their staff.

Organisational Pathology: Co-operation Between Day and Night Shift Management

Lack of communication between day and night shift management was thought to be driving a number of problems with workload, time pressures and excessive demands. Overlapping shifts between night and day management were introduced to provide an opportunity for increased co-operation and understanding between the two shifts. Monthly meetings between night and day management were also introduced.

Organisational Pathology: Harassment & Intimidation

The harassment awareness and management programme was a company-wide intervention with particular relevance to this group of staff.

Organisational Pathology: Absence Management

Across the region, 'return to work' interviews for staff returning from sick leave were introduced, but were particularly relevant to the Night Shift. A number of risk factors were linked to staff absence and the use of inexperienced staff to cover absence. Over the long term, these interviews were designed to improve absence management.

Organisational Pathology: Shift Working

To address the issue of inflexible hours, a 'swap sheet' system was introduced in stores. This would allow staff to indicate in advance when they needed cover for time off, and give them time to make arrangements with colleagues.

Organisational Pathology: Store Equipment

Funds were made available for improvements in store equipment, including the purchase and repair of stock-moving equipment. The system for arranging the repair of broken equipment was also clarified and re-communicated.

5. PHASE III: EVALUATION

5.1 PROCESS

Many interventions had only been in place for six to eight months when the evaluation was carried out in December 1998. Consequently changes were expected to be modest.

Evaluation of the interventions was carried out separately for Customer Services and Night / Evening Shift staff, both of which were based upon those used in the original risk assessment. Each instrument focused on assessing the health profile of the groups, as well as progress on the likely risk factors. An intervention inventory was also included. Following consultation, the evaluation questionnaires were amended and then agreed by the Steering Group. Distribution of the questionnaires was dealt with in the same way as in the risk assessment. The survey was supplemented by a number of structured interviews with staff from the two groups of employees. These focused on employees' reactions to the interventions. Organisational data, held both by Head Office and by the separate stores, were also examined.

40% of the Customer Services staff and 39% of the Night / Evening Shift staff returned completed questionnaires. Demographic details provided by the respondents indicated that in terms of their age, length of service, gender, and the stores worked in, those completing the evaluation survey were similar to the employees involved in the original risk assessment.

5.2 RESULTS

5.2.1 Customer Services Staff

Differences Between 1997 and 1998

In 1998, Customer Services staff felt, on average, less 'worn out' but slightly more 'tense' than at the time of the original risk assessment. However, their scores on both measures compared favourably with normative data. Within the health profile, the most noticeable change was in the percentage of staff who reported work-related musculoskeletal pain, with a drop of 24% (from 60% to 36%). There was also a slight drop in the number who intended to leave their job (from 40% to 30%). Overall, job satisfaction remained moderate to high, and absence low.

There were a number of changes in their expert judgements on the design and management of their work. For example, 46% fewer staff reported excessive demands to answer the telephone, fewer were dissatisfied with their training, fewer reported excessive interruptions, and fewer had difficulties with the available space at their work stations. There were also positive changes in reports on time pressures, demands, consultation, harassment and intimidation, appreciation and performance monitoring. Whilst encouraging, there was some variation in findings across the stores involved. It was necessary to check for variations in the implementation, awareness and impact of interventions. Therefore, the data on the penetration and impact of interventions were relevant to the evaluation process.

Organisational Penetration & Impact of the Interventions

The impact of the interventions was judged by comparing staff who were aware of, or involved in the interventions with those who were not. Where possible, comparisons were also made between staff who reported that their jobs had changed as a result of the interventions and the remainder of the staff.

Communication & Problem Solving

45% of the group reported that they knew about, had been involved in, or affected by the staff meetings with Customer Services management. However, there was a mixed response to these meetings. The number of staff reporting that the change had improved their work was equal to the number who said their work was worse as a result. More staff (60%) were aware of the monthly management meetings, and half reported that this had improved their work. Unfortunately, only a small proportion of Customer Services staff were aware of the Store Managers' Open Surgeries.

Those staff who were involved in or affected by the staff meetings were less likely to report problems with participation and consultation in decisions. There was a perception amongst staff that the meetings were beneficial in terms of discussing problems and concerns. However, the post-evaluation interviews indicated that there were practical constraints on the number of staff who could take time off from their job to attend. Some staff felt 'left out'.

> *"These meetings are held, but not all Customer Services staff can attend because there are so many of them"*

> *"These meetings have improved communication.... More people are coming forward with their ideas"*

The Store Newsletter was noticed, and received positively. 91% of the group were aware of the Newsletter, and nearly half felt that it had made their conditions at work better. Part of the positive contribution of the Store Newsletter was felt in terms of increased appreciation by the Company. Those staff who indicated that it made a positive difference to their work were more likely to report that appreciation of their efforts was adequate.

> *"The Newsletter is quite informative - you find out things that are happening in the company and the store. It brings you up to date, so you know what's going on.... It gets people involved, it broadens awareness"*

Visible & Varied Role

52% of the group reported that they knew about, had been directly involved in, or affected by the introduction of a separate Customer Services desk. Just over half of those affected attributed improvements in their job to this change. The time management courses had reached only a very small number of staff.

Work Equipment

Since only some staff spent significant periods of time on checkouts, the impact of the introduction of new checkout chairs was greater than expected. 60% of the group reported that they were aware of the change, and 58% of these reported that it had made their conditions at work better. Improvements in store equipment (e.g. more stationery, bigger desks) were reported by 60% of the group, and 59% of these felt that they had improved their working conditions.

Those staff who were aware of improvements in store equipment were less likely to report being dissatisfied with their job. The change appeared to have impacted upon the availability of equipment, one of the problems directly identified in the risk assessment. Many of the staff interviewed during the evaluation reported that there had been significant improvements in equipment.

> *"There's been new checkout chairs, and 6 new L-shapes, some of the old ones have been got rid of. The new desk has made life a lot easier."*

Harassment & Intimidation

Some other interventions went largely unnoticed. The 'Buddy System' only applied to new Customer Services staff and few people had begun work over the intervention period. Changes in the customer complaints policy were noticed by about a third of staff, with the majority of these reporting that the intervention had made no difference to their work. Only a handful were aware of the harassment awareness and management programme, which was aimed at a more senior management level.

Perhaps because of its relevance to their particular circumstances and experiences, those staff who knew about, or were affected by, the harassment awareness and management programme were more likely to report being harassed at work. Those staff who were aware of the changes in customer complaints policy were more likely to report they had less time for record paperwork and stock replenishment. It was reported by one store manager that:

> *"Staff don't like taking ownership when dealing with customers' complaints"*

5.2.2 Night / Evening Shift Staff

Differences Between 1997 and 1998

In 1998, the Night Shift staff reported feeling, on average, less 'worn out' but more 'tense' than at the time of the original risk assessment. This brought their 'worn out' scores more into line with national averages. 'Tense' scores had not risen markedly. Disappointingly, a large percentage still reported work-related musculoskeletal pain. However, fewer staff were dissatisfied with their job overall (a drop of 24% in the number reporting dissatisfaction). The number wanting to leave their job and the level of absence remained steady. The short period of time over which the interventions had been in place may have contributed to these 'headline' findings.

Progress was made on a number of the likely risk factors and other major stressors. 22% fewer staff reported that control over time pressures and encouragement for sharing work problems were inadequate. 21% fewer staff reported that time pressures were a problem. Similar changes were observed in judgements about the feedback on performance from managers, and support from work about home problems. 27% fewer staff reported that a lack of flexibility in working hours was a problem. Problems which emerged with the reorganisation of work into teams appeared to have settled: 31% fewer staff reported that the changes it brought about were problems. There was also positive movement on issues surrounding the level of interest within the job, the appraisal process, consultation, work equipment, and communication. Overall, however, reported levels of harassment and intimidation remained unchanged.

Organisational Penetration & Impact of the Interventions

Generally, awareness of the interventions was not as high as the organisation had hoped. Key contacts within the organisation reported that Night / Evening Shift staff were a difficult group to reach.

Problem Solving & Communication

Only about a third of staff were aware of the 'Open Surgeries' with Store Managers. Around half were aware of the monthly management meetings, with a third reporting that the intervention had improved their job. Those staff who were involved in, or affected by, this intervention were less likely to report a lack of participation or consideration in decision making. They were also less likely to report a lack of appreciation, inadequate support from store management, and poor communication about new procedures. Scores on 'worn out' and 'tense' measures were also lower for those aware of the intervention.

Despite a mixed reaction, those staff who were aware of the monthly management meetings were less likely to report being dissatisfied with their job overall. Those who said the meetings had improved their work were more likely to report adequate levels of participation in decision-making, and appreciation from, and communication with, their manager.

The Store Newsletter appeared to reach the group. 78% of staff reported that they knew about, had been involved in, or affected by the Store Newsletter. 35% of these staff indicated that it had made a positive contribution to their work. Staff who were unaware of the Store Newsletter were more likely to be dissatisfied with their job. Those who knew about it were less likely to report problems with management communication and appreciation of their work. There was a perception amongst those staff interviewed during the evaluation that the Store Newsletter was informative and had improved communication at all levels within their store:

> "The Store Newsletter is quite witty, but it is also serious and includes issues such as attendance. There's some stuff in there you wouldn't know about otherwise."

Co-operation Between Day & Night / Evening Shift Management

The overlapping shifts and meetings between night and day shift management received a mixed reception. Awareness was moderate: about 50% of staff were aware of the interventions. Only about 25% said that it had made their job better.

Staff who were aware of the overlapping shifts between night and day management were less likely to report high 'worn out' scores. Those who were aware of the management meetings between day and night management were less likely to report work-related musculoskeletal pain. As would be expected, for those who were aware of the intervention, communication between day and night shift management was less likely to be a problem. Feedback about, and appreciation of, the efforts of shift staff were also viewed more positively by those aware of the intervention.

Store Equipment

Disappointingly, improvements in equipment had been noticed by only about a third of staff, though many of those said their work was better as a result. There was some evidence that the changes that staff were aware of resulted from improved equipment maintenance and repair.

Those staff who were aware of improvements in store equipment tended to indicate that the availability of equipment was acceptable. Improvements in the job were linked to improved availability and maintenance of equipment, and more actions by management when equipment was reported as being damaged.

> "The trolleys we use are still quite poor, but at least we now know how to get them fixed. It will take a bit of time before we get all the equipment we really need".

115

Harassment & Intimidation / Absence Management / Shift Working

About one in four staff were aware of the training for managers on the recognition and management of harassment and intimidation. Around a third of the staff were aware of the introduction of swap sheets to stores that did not already have them. An awareness of this training programme was linked to the reporting of adequate support from store management and low 'worn out' scores. Around half the staff were aware of 'return to work' interviews. Few staff attributed changes in their working conditions to these interventions.

Commentary: Customer Services Staff and Night / Evening Shift

Bearing in mind that the interventions were only in place for a short period of time, these results were received as encouraging. Although further work needed to be done to address stressors within the organisation, significant progress was made during the case study.

6. LEARNING POINTS

6.1 CHAMPION

Having a 'champion' within an organisation who will highlight the importance of the project to management certainly facilitates the progression of the project. In this case study, all stages progressed relatively quickly and easily due largely to the strong commitment of the Occupational Health Manager. The Occupational Health Manager initiated contact with the project team and did much to emphasise the importance of the project to managers within the organisation.

6.2 SURVEY DISTRIBUTION

It is best to ensure that, wherever possible, distribution and completion of questionnaires is undertaken during work time. Using this strategy, a reasonable response rate was achieved despite the large geographical spread of the employees in this project. Selling this strategy to management can be challenging. The potential benefits of the project (in terms of improved working conditions and more efficient working) can be used to justify some disruption. Of course, the risk assessment should be designed and carried out in a way that minimises such disruption.

6.3 COMMITMENT FROM THE TOP

Commitment to the project from the Board of Directors ensured that the project was seen as a priority by middle managers, who, in turn, played a key role in driving the project through to completion. The results of the risk assessment were fed back to the Board, who expressed their interest and commitment to ensuring that interventions would be carried out and evaluated.

6.4 LOCAL MANAGEMENT SUPPORT

Involving the Store Managers in all aspects of the project was vital to the design, implementation and success of interventions. It was anticipated that many of the interventions would only work with local commitment and support. Store Managers were the only staff who could provide this. Of course, levels of commitment and opportunities to implement interventions varied from store to store, and these factors contributed to the unevenness of the impact of the interventions. In most companies, local management support will be necessary for the success of any interventions.

CASE STUDY 3

CHEMICAL PROCESS STAFF

1. SUMMARY

This case study involved employees working for a large chemical manufacturing firm in the north of England. The project focused on one of its manufacturing groups which produced industrial chemicals using three chemical manufacturing processes. Within the manufacturing group, the working conditions of two groups of staff were examined: 65 process operators (shift workers) and 35 managerial and professional staff. Together they represented the majority of the workforce in the group. The project was carried out over a period of two and a half years.

1.1 PHASE I: RISK ASSESSMENT

Both groups of staff appeared to be relatively satisfied with most aspects of their work. Their reporting of symptoms of being 'worn out' and 'tense' compared well with national averages. Absence levels were low and few staff wanted to leave the company. The incidence of work-related musculoskeletal pain was moderate to low for both groups of staff, particularly considering the nature of the work carried out by the process operators.

Despite these encouraging findings, management and employee representatives were keen to improve working conditions further by intervening to tackle any stressors and likely risk factors that could be found in the risk assessment data. Those aspects of work identified and targeted for intervention were:

- Unpleasant environmental conditions and poor equipment in some areas of the manufacturing plant

- Incidents of harassment and intimidation

- Problems with performance monitoring, appraisal, career development and bonus allocation

- Inadequate communication with senior management outside the plant and perceived lack of job security

- Lack of consultation over plant equipment

- The impact of shift work on home life

- Inadequate development of skills

- The complexity of promotions procedures

- High workload and lack of control over time pressures

1.2 PHASE II: TRANSLATION AND RISK REDUCTION

Many interventions came about through the efforts of the Steering Group working with the group's Manufacturing Manager. Some changes had been planned prior to the project, with the project acting as a catalyst for their introduction. The organisational pathology of the stressors and risk factors was quickly identified. Site-wide initiatives were also put into action to address some of the problem areas. Many interventions were the direct result of Steering Group discussions. Taking all these influences together the package of interventions included:

- A programme to raise safety awareness and provide local solutions to equipment and environment problems

- An awareness programme on harassment and intimidation at work

- Bonus allocation and appraisal training for managers, coupled with extra appraisal and development meetings

- Introduction of personal development learning objectives, better use of English, and individual ownership of objectives in appraisals

- Quicker delivery of training (with new training facilities), refresher training, and more emergency exercises

- Strategy teams to address shift-work and workload issues

1.3 PHASE III: EVALUATION

During the intervention period, other manufacturing groups on the site were out-sourced to external companies and job losses occurred. Consequently, there was an increase in job insecurity across the site. Further, there was a period of reduced demand for the goods produced by the manufacturing group. Inevitably such events impacted on the effectiveness of interventions. Despite this backdrop, some positive findings emerged. These were:

- High awareness of key interventions, particularly among the managerial and professional staff

- Positive reactions to a number of the interventions

- Evidence that those employees affected by the interventions viewed their work more positively than those not affected by them

- Evidence of more positive well-being among those exposed to the interventions

The positive findings from the risk assessment were generally maintained through the evaluation stage.

2. BACKGROUND

The company involved in this case study was a large multinational which produced chemicals and petroleum based products. It has a number of major sites across the UK, including one in the north of England that specialises in the production of macro chemicals for the manufacturing sector. This site was divided (both geographically and organisationally) according to the type of chemicals produced. The manufacturing group involved in this project supported three chemical production processes.

Two of these processes were fairly modern and had benefited from significant investment in recent years. Plant machinery and related equipment had been updated, and processes were controlled using touch-screen or other computer-based technologies. Although these two plants were large, they were staffed by only four or five process operators at any one time. These employees could be involved in the computer control of the processes, but also worked on the plant (taking samples, operating valves, and running checks on equipment). Some employees operated machinery which bagged and stored the finished product. The third chemical process was far older and smaller, and consisted of two manufacturing units, one of which was staffed by one employee. The control rooms were partly computerised but, at the time of the risk assessment, other instrumentation was old and unreliable, and the plant equipment extremely dirty. This chemical process was messy and the work was physical, with much stair climbing and manual work. The chemical produced had fairly low profit margins and, hence, investment in plant equipment had been low.

A number of professional groups were involved in the running of the three processes. These staff were mainly engineers, but also included a small group of managers and supervisors who managed the day-to-day running of the processes. The manufacturing group was a strong financial performer, and while profit margins on the end products were low, market share was high. However, the group was seen as the 'poor relation' on the site, since other processes on the site produced more expensive chemicals with higher profit margins. Many workers were of the opinion that the manufacturing group had not received its fair share of recognition and investment over recent years. At the start of the risk assessment in 1996, there was some concern that demand for the chemicals produced by the group was likely to dip in the near future.

In 1994, the site had been de-unionised. This had a number of implications, including the introduction of a common set of terms and conditions and a move away from union negotiated pay rises. Individual performance contracts were introduced with bonus payments calculated through performance evaluation and appraisal. The site had also been through a benchmarking process which evaluated the contribution of each individual to the business. This resulted in some job losses, mostly through early retirement.

Contact was made with the organisation through the site Health and Safety Advisor in the summer of 1995. Agreement to proceed was secured from the manufacturing group's manager late in that year. The manufacturing group had been identified as being fairly typical of manufacturing groups across the site, and it was envisaged that results from the project would be useful to the other similar manufacturing groups. The Steering Group set up to guide the project included an employee representative, the manufacturing group's Manufacturing Manager, and representatives from Personnel, Occupational Health and Health and Safety.

3. PHASE I: RISK ASSESSMENT

3.1 PROCESS

The first phase of the risk assessment involved a thorough period of familiarisation with the working practices and working conditions of the two groups of employees. It was important to understand the complexities of the plant and of the work. Fifteen Work Analysis Interviews were carried out, involving employees from each of the three chemical processes and both groups of staff. The Familiarisation phase involved workplace observation, tours of the manufacturing processes and examination of organisational data. Ten Management Systems Audit Interviews were conducted with key stakeholders. These data were combined to construct the Work Environment Survey. The Steering Group had a major input into the questionnaire design phase.

The risk assessment questionnaire was distributed in April 1996, and was collected during a confidential one-to-one interview with each employee. The use of this interview-based strategy yielded an extremely high response rate of 85%.

3.2 RESULTS

The health profile of both groups of employees compared favourably to other groups involved in similar work (see Figure 1 below). Process operators reported being slightly less 'worn out', but far less 'tense' than comparable groups of employees. Given the relatively physical nature of their work, the proportion of process operators reporting musculoskeletal pain (42%) was relatively low. Self reported absence was low (3 days/year), with job satisfaction being relatively high. The vast majority of process operators wanted to stay in the company. A similar picture emerged for the professional and managerial groups, although (as was expected given the type of work they did) their 'tense' and 'worn out' scores were higher, and the incidence of musculoskeletal pain was lower (32%).

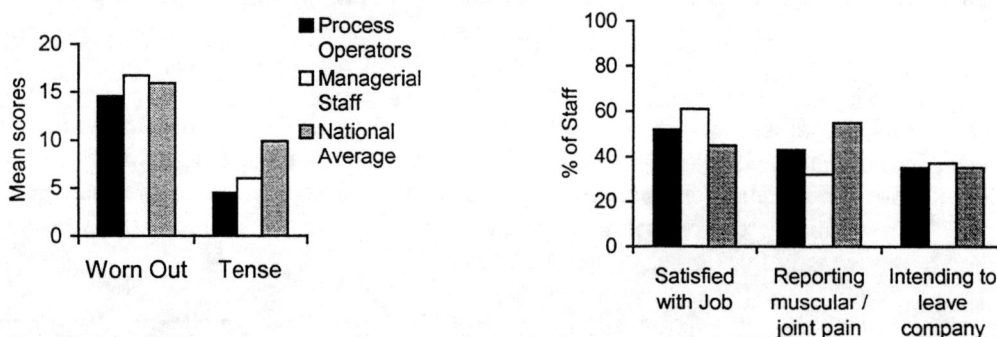

Figure 1: Evaluating organisational and individual health

The Work Environment Survey revealed that staff were relatively satisfied with many aspects of their work, such as their working relationships with colleagues, the amount of variety in their work, and the length and predictability of working hours.

Despite these encouraging findings, it emerged that the Steering Group were keen to tackle any stressors or risk factors that could be uncovered in the risk assessment data, even if exposure to these problems was relatively low. Even with encouraging overall results, they may mask at least some staff reporting poor well-being and some problems with the design and management of work. While acknowledging the positive nature of the risk assessment results, subsequent discussions focused on addressing the small number of stressors and likely risk factors. These were:

Process Operators

- Unpleasant contact with chemicals and poor working environments
- Lack of cleanliness around plant equipment, and lack of consultation about changes and improvements to equipment
- Poor quality and infrequent appraisals and problems with performance monitoring
- High bonuses being unobtainable, and unfair bonus allocation
- Poor communication plant-wide and with company senior management
- Lack of career prospects and personal development opportunities
- The impact of shift-work on home life
- Some staff reporting harassment and intimidation, job insecurity, and high workload

Managerial, Professional and Supervisory Staff

- Lack of control over workload and time pressures
- Unfair bonus allocation
- Unpleasant contact with chemicals
- Lack of staff and high workload
- Complex promotional procedures, and inadequate opportunities to develop skills

4. PHASE II: TRANSLATION AND RISK REDUCTION

The results of the risk assessment were presented to the Steering Group in July 1996. All employees in the two groups received a three-page briefing which included the key findings. The Steering Group had anticipated positive results, but they were keen to focus on areas warranting further improvement. At an early stage, it became apparent that some problem areas were governed by site-wide structures (e.g. the shift work patterns and promotion procedures) and could not be changed by the Steering Group. Encouragingly, most of these issues were recognised by the company and were being investigated by strategy teams and focus Groups. These had been set up to address issues identified in recent employee opinion surveys, and were working to devise solutions to a number of relevant problems. However, it appeared that interventions to tackle the other issues could be designed and implemented by the Steering Group.

Within the Steering Group, the Manufacturing Manager drove the intervention design with specialist support. Employee participation was patchy, since, for various reasons, attendance by the employee representative was irregular. An action plan was devised that focused on four underlying issues: harassment, appraisal and reward, training and development, and environmental conditions. The Manufacturing Manager also worked independently with colleagues and other on-site groups on a number of other interventions. These focused on addressing the issues raised by the process operators, but which involved professional and managerial groups in their implementation.

INTERVENTION PACKAGE

Organisational Pathology: Environmental Conditions

Championed by the Manufacturing Manager, various actions were designed to address safety issues and environmental conditions on the plant. Activities included interviewing staff about safety procedures, consulting staff about plant equipment, improved housekeeping procedures, enhanced accident and near miss reporting, and a greater investment in plant equipment.

Organisational Pathology: Harassment and Intimidation

A harassment and awareness intimidation programme. Cross-functional focus groups were run within the manufacturing group to identify the behaviours that employees believed represented harassment and intimidation. Findings from the focus groups were translated into a training package that was delivered within the manufacturing group, and site-wide (with the appropriate modifications). Tackling intimidation and harassment were also made key issues at management meetings and management away-days within the manufacturing group.

Organisational Pathology: Training and Development

A package of measures to improve training quality and delivery arising out of workshops to investigate training issues across the plant. A dedicated trainer for the group was also appointed to support an enhanced training structure. Measures taken included planning and time commitment for immediate training upon the installation of new equipment, introduction of computer based training facilities to allow employees to train off-line, refresher training for process staff, simulated emergency exercises to allow staff to familiarise themselves with emergency procedures, and the cessation of the practice of cancelling dedicated training days to free employees to cover for colleagues absent or on holiday.

Development of the performance appraisal process. This included the introduction of team and peer appraisal, refresher courses and appraiser workshops for managers and staff, and the use of clearer English in appraisal documents. The frequency of appraisal was also increased, with the introduction of two extra 'development discussions' (designed to explore progress more frequently, and informally and review development needs). Within formal appraisal sessions, appraisers were guided to shift the ownership of objectives to employees (rather than enforce them top-down) and build flexibility into objectives to reflect changes in the job. To enhance the appraisal process it was decided that a learning or training objective should be agreed at formal appraisal sessions. This was designed to increase opportunities for staff to use and develop their skills and abilities.

Organisational Pathology: Reward Systems

Measures to improve bonus allocation. This included a series of meetings at senior and middle management level to discuss best practice in bonus allocation. The issue was made a priority at management away-days. Guidelines were also produced to indicate that bonuses should be weighted on the performance in the core job rather than extra jobs taken on by some employees. Managers were also advised to make more use of by the event bonuses to reward specific instances of outstanding performance when appropriate.

5. PHASE III: EVALUATION

5.1 METHOD

Evaluating the impact of interventions in this organisation was challenging. The positive results from the risk assessment suggested that any improvements would be modest at best. Further, in the year prior to the risk assessment, the manufacturing site had entered a period of uncertainty, with other production groups on the site being out-sourced to external organisations. The evaluation revealed that a large number of staff believed the future of this manufacturing group to be insecure.

Changes occurring over the period of the intervention were measured using an abridged version of the risk assessment questionnaire which focused on the stressors and likely risk factors. Employees were also asked to indicate their awareness of, involvement in, and reaction to, the interventions designed by the Steering Group, and to the site-wide changes and initiatives.

The evaluation questionnaire was distributed in November 1998, after it had been agreed with the Steering Group. As with the risk assessment, confidential one-to-one interviews with each employee were arranged to facilitate the collection of completed questionnaires. 63% of the questionnaires were returned. Although the response rate was lower than for the original survey, those returning questionnaires appeared to be representative of the groups of workers being studied. In terms of age, gender, job title, length of service, and chemical process worked on, the groups were highly similar to those assessed in 1996.

5.2 RESULTS

Differences Between 1996 and 1998

There were some changes in staff perceptions of their work that, at first sight, appeared to be related to aspects of the intervention package. In addition, the positive aspects of work revealed by the original risk assessment were also strongly endorsed in the 1998 survey.

Among process operators, a smaller proportion of staff were dissatisfied with cleanliness around the plant. While over half reported this as a problem in 1996, less than a third reported it as a problem in 1998. There were more modest improvements in perceptions of plant temperature, and consultation about changes in equipment. Compared with 1996, 20% fewer staff reported that contact with chemicals was unpleasant.

The proportion of process operators reporting dissatisfaction with personal development opportunities and the regularity of formal appraisals had fallen. A greater proportion of staff were also satisfied that their personal objectives were achievable. In 1996, harassment and intimidation was reported by 25% of the process operators. In 1998, this figure was 15%.

As expected, at the end of the project, a greater proportion of process operators were dissatisfied with their job security (a rise of 17% to 55%). Many more were dissatisfied with the promotion system (up from 48% to 71%), the impact of work on home life (up from 21% to 39%) and demands to provide cover for those absent or on leave (up from 22% to 37%). Key stakeholders reported that little had actually been done to change the promotion system over the intervention period, and that the more able employees were becoming increasingly frustrated. There were also more demands to cover for colleagues who were absent or on leave. In part, this arose because of management's commitment not to cancel training days in order to provide cover. At the time of the original risk assessment, it was reported that training days were often cancelled at short notice so that employees could cover for absent colleagues. Management's commitment that employees would not be taken off training courses meant that more often, cover was provided through overtime or the swapping of shifts. One other unexpected result was that a far greater proportion of process operators were reporting problems with the level of demands from their manager (up to 45% from just 4%).

Similar findings emerged for the managerial and professional staff. The proportion reporting inadequate job security had increased to 37%. However, 15% fewer reported problems with the fairness of bonus allocation, and there were large drops in the proportion of staff reporting unpleasant contact with chemical substances. Only a handful of employees reported these as problems at evaluation. More staff reported that control over workload was satisfactory, and that staffing levels were adequate. Generally this group of staff reported few stressors associated with their work.

The overall health profile of the process operators remained fairly stable across the intervention period despite the prevailing atmosphere of job insecurity. 'Worn out' and 'tense' scores remained low, with little discernible change. Absence had increased slightly but remained low. However, job satisfaction had decreased, with 15% fewer reporting overall satisfaction with their job. 50% reported wanting to leave their job in 1998, compared with 34% in 1996. However, actual turnover remained negligible. Encouragingly, the proportion of process operators reporting work-related musculoskeletal pain had dropped to 34%, a low figure given the nature of the work. The good health profile of managerial and professional staff was maintained. 'Worn out' and 'tense' scores dropped to levels that compared well with national averages. Only one in four reported work-related musculoskeletal pain. Absence was low at one day per year. Job satisfaction remained high (53% satisfied).

Organisational Penetration and Impact of the Interventions

It was inevitable that job insecurity would have an impact on the awareness of, and reactions to, the interventions. However, a general picture emerged that suggested that the locally-based interventions had been noticed and had an impact on the work of both groups. Managerial and professional staff were more aware of the interventions based around performance appraisal and communication than were the process operators.

In order to investigate the impact of each intervention, employees who had experienced or been affected by the interventions were compared to those who had not experienced or been positively affected by the interventions. Unfortunately, because only nineteen managerial, supervisory and professional staff returned the evaluation questionnaire, it was not possible to describe the impact of each intervention for this group, and the following analysis concerns process operators.

Environmental Conditions
The highest awareness levels were for the initiatives on environmental conditions. All process operators were at least aware of it, and 66% had been directly involved or affected in some way by the resulting changes occurring. The intervention was very positively received, with 55% of the process operators attributing improvements in their work to the intervention. 66% of the managerial and professional staff attributed improvements in their job to the intervention. For the process operators, this initiative appeared to associated with a number of positive evaluations of work and well-being. Those who had been involved were more likely to report that staffing levels within their work area were adequate. Those who believed that their work had improved as a result of the intervention were also more likely to report that the procedures for monitoring their performance were adequate, and to be satisfied with their job overall.

Harassment and Intimidation

Awareness of the harassment and intimidation awareness programme was relatively low among process operators. 44% were aware of the programme, but only a handful of staff reported having been involved in it, or affected by it. Similar results were reported by the managerial and professional staff. Unsurprisingly, barely any staff reported that the intervention had made their work better. However, the effects of this programme were expected to knock-on in terms of subtle changes in behaviour and culture. Although any changes could not be directly attributed to the intervention, 17 employees (20%) reported either harassment or intimidation in 1996, while only 7 employees (12%) reported harassment or intimidation in 1998.

Training & Development

The measures to improve training quality and delivery were noticed by a large proportion of process operators. The results of the evaluation indicated that many staff had been directly involved in, or affected by, these changes. The immediate delivery of training on new equipment had been noticed by 75% of the process staff, with around half of these being directly involved in that training. 36% of those who were aware of the training said it had improved their work. Those staff involved in the training were more likely to report satisfactory time pressures and control over their workload. Those who believed their job had improved as a result were also more likely to be satisfied with a number of aspects of the appraisal systems including the quality and regularity of formal appraisals, and recognition of effort. The awareness and reaction figures for managerial and professional staff were almost identical to those of the process operators.

There was a similar response to the introduction of computer-based training facilities. Again, just under half of the process operators had been affected by the training, and the majority of them said that their work had improved as a result. Staff who were involved in the use of these facilities were less likely to report problems with time pressures. Those who said that the intervention had improved their work indicated that their efforts were adequately recognised and were more likely to be satisfied with their work overall. As was expected, since the training was not aimed at their jobs, very few managerial and professional staff reported that the intervention had improved their work.

Other training initiatives appeared to be well received by process operators. 70% were aware of refresher training on their core job. Around a third of those involved in the training reported it had improved their job. Employees who had been involved in this were more likely to report being satisfied with the way their performance was monitored. Staff who indicated that the training had improved their work were less likely to report problems with unpleasant exposure to raw materials, more likely to be satisfied with the amount of control they could exert over time pressures and more likely to report adequate recognition of their efforts. Additionally, they were less likely to indicate that they wished to leave the company.

Levels of awareness of and involvement in simulation emergency exercises were similar, but over half of those involved indicated that their work had improved as a result. Staff who reported that these exercises had improved their work were more likely to report satisfaction with their personal development opportunities, and less likely to report problematic time pressures within their work.

Commitments to a set number of training days and assurances that these would not be cancelled to provide cover had been noted by 60% of process staff and 70% of the managerial and professional group. However, only a small proportion (around a quarter) of the process operators had been directly affected by the intervention. The vast majority of process operators believed that their work was no different as a result of these two interventions. These interventions were not directly relevant to the work done by most managerial and professional staff.

Most employees from both groups were aware of the introduction of training and learning objectives into appraisals, but only a few reported that their job had improved as a result. Those who did were more likely to report that their performance was adequately monitored, and that they were satisfied with their job overall. Employees who believed the intervention had made their job better were more likely to indicate that their career prospects in the external job market were good and that demands to cover colleagues' work were not excessive. Changes to the management of objectives seemed to have made more of a difference to managerial and professional staff, the majority of whom indicated that the intervention had resulted in positive changes to their job. 70% of managerial and professional staff had been involved in informal performance and development discussions and the vast majority indicated that these were a positive step forward. However, only 20% of process operators reported direct involvement in informal performance discussions.

Though most employees were aware that ownership of objectives should have increased and that objectives should have been updated, managerial and professional staff responded much more positively, with around half saying the changes had had a positive impact on their work. Only a handful of process operators reported such improvements. Those process operators who were aware of greater ownership of their personal objectives were more likely to report satisfaction with their career development prospects within the organisation, and less likely to report problems with the fairness of bonus allocation. Overall, they were also more likely to report satisfaction with their work. A similar picture emerged for those staff who were aware of updates in objectives. These employees were also more likely to indicate that appraisals were regular enough and that their efforts were adequately recognised. Disappointingly, 63% of the process operators were not aware of the use of clearer English in appraisal documents Unsurprisingly, employees who were aware of such changes in appraisal documentation were more likely to be satisfied with the objectives agreed during appraisal sessions.

Appraisal & Reward
There were mixed results for the various measures taken to improve the formal appraisal and reward process. While these were aimed at all staff, it appeared to be the managerial staff who were most affected by them. Nearly all had some experience of team and peer appraisals and over half reported that their working conditions had improved as a result. However, few indicated that the appraisal workshop had made a difference to their work. Few process operators appeared to have been involved in these interventions. Very few had been involved in team or peer appraisals. Awareness of refresher courses on the appraisal system was low (33%), and again only a small number reported that it had improved their job.

Just over half of the process operators were aware that workshops on bonus allocation had taken place, and about half of the managerial and professional staff had been involved in them. While half of the managerial and professional staff reported some improvement in their job as a result, the majority of process operators indicated that their work had not been affected. 63% of the process operators and 79% of the professional and managerial staff were aware of an increased weighting of salary increases and bonuses according to performance on the core job rather than 'extra' jobs taken on by some employees. In both groups about one in four said their job was better as a result. These findings were expected, since bonuses were still dependent on individual performance, and variations in performance were likely to affect the impact of the interventions on individuals. Those process operators who indicated that their job had improved as a result of this shift in emphasis were more likely to report satisfaction with the fairness of bonus allocation, the formal appraisal system, recognition of effort and the monitoring of performance. The other measure designed to improve bonus allocation – the increased use of 'by the event' bonuses – went unnoticed by the process operators, but around half of the managerial and professional staff indicated their job had improved as a result of the change.

Other Interventions

Process operators were aware of one other intervention introduced after the risk assessment: the monthly team brief. This was not a planned part of the intervention package. It was a meeting for managerial and process staff, held separately for each of the chemical processes. The running of the plant and related problems were discussed. The vast majority of process operators (82%) were aware of these briefs, though few had been directly involved. A third indicated the brief had improved their work. Managerial and professional staff responded much more enthusiastically with 70% indicating that their job had been improved by the briefing.

Commentary

The positive findings from the risk assessment were generally maintained through the evaluation stage. There was also evidence that well-being and satisfaction scores were most favourable for those who were affected by the interventions. At the time of writing this report work was in progress to raise awareness of some of the interventions. The results of the evaluation survey were also being used to develop further some of the interventions in order to set in motion a process of continuous improvement.

6. LEARNING POINTS

6.1 INVOLVING EMPLOYEES

Being able to draw on employee expertise was crucial at all stages of the project. However, it was difficult to do so within this organisation. Shift-work often meant that employee representatives were unable to attend Steering Group meetings. Consequently, the intervention design phase was more management-driven than it was in the other case studies in this report. However, it was still possible to involve employees by asking them to comment on management ideas and suggestions. For example, a group of employees from all sections of the plant were involved in the design of the harassment and intimidation awareness programme. Where it is logistically difficult to involve employees in initial decision making, it can be useful to gather their comments on plans for action that have already been developed.

6.2 QUESTIONNAIRE DESIGN

The work done by the two groups of staff involved in this case study was quite different. This suggested that two different versions of the Work Environment Survey would be required. However, after carrying out the initial job analysis, two pieces of information indicated that this would not, in fact, be the case. First, only a small number of problems were raised by each group of staff. Second, within these problem areas there appeared to be some common ground. Since relatively few issues had been raised, it was decided to combine them all into one version of the assessment instrument. The interviews suggested that there was enough common ground in the way both sets of employees perceived their work to allow for same item wording to be applicable to, and recognised by, both groups. This is not always the case. Interview data often indicates marked differences in perceptions of work problems, the nature of those problems and the language used to describe them within a single workplace. In such situations, the design of a number of questionnaires which reflect these differences is strongly recommended.

6.3 USING POSITIVE RESULTS

In this company, the results of the risk assessment survey were generally positive. While this indicates that there is no need for drastic action, the results can be used for development work. For both groups of employees in this project, two strong sources of satisfaction were teamwork and the challenging and varied nature of the work. These were developed in a move towards more autonomous group working, and supported by improved training arrangements. Spreading 'best practice' to other areas may be another beneficial way of using positive findings.

6.4 THE IMPACT OF INSTABILITY

The period over which the interventions were implemented was a time of considerable uncertainty for the organisation involved. Although the chemical manufacturing processes were generally profitable, the products had relatively low profit margins. The structure of the operation was formally reviewed during the intervention period. Other processes (not involved in the project) had been outsourced. These events created a great deal of uncertainty among staff. Such uncertainty could have impacted upon the results of the evaluation survey. To investigate this, employees were questioned about their views on the future of their manufacturing operation as part of the evaluation survey. Uncertainty about the future of the group was linked to dissatisfaction with bonus allocation, performance monitoring, demands from managers, career development and opportunities to use skills and abilities. It appeared that staff who were most uncertain about the future were those who did not feel they were being developed or rewarded.

6.5 TRANSFERRING RESULTS

One of the questions often asked about this type of project is how far the results apply to other groups within an organisation. In this case study, the company was keen to use the lessons learned in the project on other parts of the site. While it is advisable to carry out a risk assessment in each area, there is potential for drawing broad conclusions. For example, if the work done by another group of staff is highly similar to that carried out by the risk assessment group, there is the possibility that similar problems may need to be addressed. Organisations have a wealth of information and expertise they can draw on to investigate this possibility. In this company, the harassment and intimidation awareness programme and the initiative to improve environmental conditions were spread to other chemical manufacturing process on the site.

CASE STUDY 4

SEWAGE TREATMENT WORKS STAFF

1. SUMMARY

This study was carried out among two groups of employees from the Waste Water section of a Utilities Company. The two groups involved were Support staff (administrative and managerial staff, project co-ordinators and office based technical specialists) at a single Sewage Treatment Works, and the Operational, Maintenance and Sewerage staff (manual workers) based at a number of sewage treatment sites.

1.1 PHASE I: RISK ASSESSMENT

The risk assessment was carried out in September 1997. Different versions of the Work Environment Survey were tailored to the needs and contexts of the two groups.

Support Staff

These employees had a fairly good health profile in comparison to similar work groups and national norms. The one negative finding was that their job dissatisfaction was relatively high. The risk assessment isolated a number of issues that were identified by Support Staff as major stressors. Some of these proved to be likely risk factors. These included:

- Time pressures and a high workload
- Poor communication and difficulties in working with corporate systems
- Other staff appearing to know little about the work done by Support staff
- Physical risks (in particular long periods of computer work)
- Perceived poor job security
- Lack of participation in strategic decisions
- A lack of understanding of the purpose and value of the work done
- Long commuting times

Operational, Maintenance and Sewerage Staff

These employees reported feeling more 'worn out' and 'tense' than many comparable groups of manual workers, and reported relatively high levels of job dissatisfaction. However, the incidence of musculoskeletal pain was not as high as might have been expected for manual work. A number of major stressors and likely risk factors were identified for this group. These were:

- A cluster of issues related to time pressures

- Inadequate performance monitoring

- Low pay

- Poor communication across many levels

- Issues surrounding organisational change

- Problems with contractors' health and safety performance

- Inadequate training and problems with team working

- Other employees knowing little about the work done by support staff

1.2 PHASE II: TRANSLATION AND RISK REDUCTION

Feedback on the results from the risk assessment was used mainly to inform ongoing and future changes. Most changes were implemented early in 1998. The main interventions were:

- Setting up of a Business Committee between management and trade union representatives, communication of the results of the Employee Opinion Survey to staff, and the introduction of a Meetings Etiquette

- Management training and development initiatives

- Introduction of one-to-one performance reviews and 360 degree appraisals (the use of colleague, supervisor, and subordinate ratings in the appraisal process)

- Opportunities for home working with increased availability of laptops

- Auditing of health and safety standards of contractors, and 'spot checks'

1.3 PHASE III: EVALUATION

The evaluation was carried out in November 1998, which allowed only a relatively short intervention period. The results identified:

- High levels of awareness and involvement in the interventions

- Some improvements in Operational, Maintenance and Sewerage staff's feelings of being 'worn out' and 'tense'

- Evidence of positive impact associated with a number of interventions in terms of well-being and employees' reports on the adequacy of working conditions

Given the climate of continuous organisational change in which the case study was carried out, these results were encouraging. However, for a number of reasons, some issues were not addressed by the intervention package. Therefore it was recommended that problems remaining after the evaluation be carefully monitored and where possible subsequently tackled.

2. BACKGROUND

The Utilities Company involved in this case study provides water services for over seven million customers and wastewater services for nearly 12 million customers in the UK. The company was privatised in 1989, and has since undergone a number of organisational changes, particularly in relation to its sewage treatment services. One major change was a move towards a more flexible, multiskilled workforce. Multiskilling was introduced in 1993, an initiative that aimed to remove traditional trade-based demarcation barriers and improve teamwork. Other recent changes within the sewage treatment services included the outsourcing of part of the Maintenance division, and a move towards a programme of 'performance management' with the introduction of performance related pay, and, since April 1998, appraisals or 'performance reviews' for each employee. The Company was concerned about the effects that such changes might have on the well-being of employees. This was one of the main drivers behind the identification of Waste Water as a suitable group for involvement in the risk management project. There had also been a reduction in the workforce over recent years, which had included involuntary redundancies. A review of staffing levels took place during the period of the risk management project, and created some uncertainty about the future job security among those involved in the risk assessment.

The case study was carried out with two groups of employees:

The first group was Support staff at a single Sewage Treatment Works, who were involved in a variety of office based jobs. The majority of these employees were involved in business administration and operational planning.

The second group was Operational, Maintenance and Sewerage staff who were based at a number of Sewage Treatment sites around the company's 'catchment area'. Generally, these were skilled manual workers who were involved in the running and maintenance of the waste water systems. Most of these employees were process operators at sewage treatment works. The majority of the employees in this group were involved in the maintenance of sewage works. A small proportion of these staff were involved in the inspection and maintenance of the sewage systems that served homes and industrial sites.

The Steering Group included representatives from sewage treatment services management, Occupational Health, Health and Safety, the trade unions representative, and representatives of the various groups of employees involved in the risk assessments.

3. PHASE I: RISK ASSESSMENT

3.1 PROCESS

The project was widely publicised at the sites involved. The Familiarisation stage was extensive and involved visits and workplace observations of staff at all the sewage treatment works involved. Several sources of data held by the organisation proved useful, particularly health and safety policies and procedures which revealed much about the variety and complexity of work carried out by the manual workers involved. Much of the information gathered was used to inform the design of the Work Environment Survey. Work Analysis Interviews were conducted with 25 staff from the two groups. As was expected, analysis of interviews and other data resulted in the design of two assessment questionnaires that reflecting the different profiles of issues reported by office staff and manual workers. However, it was decided that there was sufficient common ground within the issues raised by operational, maintenance and sewerage staff to justify the construction of a single questionnaire for this group. The risk assessment was carried out in September 1997, using questionnaires agreed by the Steering Group. The Steering Group agreed to title the project: 'The Occupational Stress Review'.

The questionnaires were distributed to the home addresses of all members of the two groups. Managers were previously asked to brief their teams about the objectives of the project, and to notify them that they would be receiving an assessment questionnaire. The objectives of the assessment were described to the respondents in a covering letter from the project team. They were told to telephone either the project champion in Occupational Health, or the researchers if they had any questions. Respondents were able to return completed surveys in a pre-paid envelope, either via a collection box on site, or directly to the project team via the postal service. Unfortunately, only a low response rate was achieved, and managers were asked, once again, to encourage their teams to complete the questionnaire. As a result, the overall response rate increased to 52% for Support Staff and to 21% for Operational, Maintenance and Sewerage staff.

3.2 RESULTS

3.2.1 Support Staff

The health profile reported by this group indicated that their 'worn out' scores were similar to those reported by comparable groups of office workers. Their 'tense' scores were lower than those typically reported by comparable groups. Similar positive results were found in terms of high levels of job satisfaction and low levels of sickness absence. Few within the group wished to leave the company. Health related behaviours compared well with national data for office based workers.

However, despite these positive findings, the Steering Group were keen to improve working conditions further by tackling a number of the major stressors and likely risk factors identified. These were:

- A lack of job security

- A lack of understanding of the purpose and value of their team's contribution

- Too much time spent travelling to work

- High workload, time pressures, deadlines, and frequent interruptions

- Lack of communication with senior management, lack of participation in strategic decisions

- Other staff and customers not understanding the work done by Support Staff

- Inadequate opportunities for rest breaks

- Poor quality of corporate systems, e.g. databases

- Lack of protection from physical risks associated with VDU use

3.2.2 Operational, Maintenance and Sewerage Staff

Comparing the health profile of this group of employees to other manual workers revealed higher scores on measures of feeling 'worn out' and 'tense'. Job satisfaction was also relatively low. However, health related behaviours were in line with national data for manual workers, and the incidence of musculoskeletal pain was not exceptionally high. The proportion wishing to leave the company was moderate.

A number of major stressors were reported by this group, and a number of likely risk factors were identified. These were:

- Heavy time pressures and tight deadlines

- Inadequate monitoring of performance and feedback from management

- Perceived lack of fairness in the grading system

- Other staff not being aware of what the job done by the group involved

- Poor communication with, and a lack of appreciation from senior management

- High levels of organisational change and poor handling of redundancies

- Contractors failing to meet company requirements on health and safety

- Lack of encouragement to attend training courses and to work in teams

- Perceived poor planning and organisation at senior management level

4. PHASE II: TRANSLATION AND RISK REDUCTION

The results from the risk assessment were fed back to the Steering Group in November 1997 and were well received. Using a number of planning aids, underlying problems were identified and detailed action plans were drawn up. For support staff underlying pathologies related to systems of communication with senior management, to demands associated with meetings, to training and development systems and to the home-work interface. For operational, maintenance and sewerage staff, three 'pathologies' were identified that were amenable to intervention: communications with senior management, training and development, and the systems for the auditing of health and safety compliance. The packages of interventions included was devised over a full day of discussions. Responsibilities and timescales were laid out in detail to ensure that interventions were not 'lost' within the organisation. To support this, a detailed plan of action was drawn up and progress reviewed at regular intervals over the period between implementation and evaluation. Some interventions were applicable to both groups of staff.

INTERVENTION PACKAGE 1
Support Staff

Organisational Pathology: Communication Systems

The setting up of a Business Committee for management and trade union representatives. The meetings were designed so that management were able to keep the trade unions informed of the challenges facing the company and the sewage treatment services. This was designed to improve communication, and address some concerns over job security.

The results of the Employee Opinion Survey were re-communicated to all staff through focus groups and meetings. This was targeted at improving communication, but also aimed to demonstrate that senior managers were aware of the difficulties facing staff.

Organisational Pathology: Training and Development Systems

Management Training and Development was strengthened to allow managers to enhance their skills and expertise through training and assessment e.g. National Vocational Qualifications.

Appraisals, or one-to-one reviews, for all staff with their line manager were introduced to lay out clearer career structures and ensure that feedback was given to staff at regular intervals.

Organisational Pathology: Demands of Meetings

A Meetings Etiquette was introduced, comprising a list of requirements for holding effective meetings e.g. 'choosing' convenient locations for all, establishing a chairperson, keeping minutes, not interrupting a speaker, etc. The list was forwarded to all staff via E-mail, and was made into a poster and placed in all meeting rooms at all sites. The Steering Group felt that a number of the problems surrounding time pressures resulted from poorly run meetings that did not keep to agendas, and failed to reach decisions or produce action.

Organisational Pathology: Home – work Interface

Extended opportunities for home working were made available, with the increased availability of laptops. This was targeted to reduce problems with commuting to work.

INTERVENTION PACKAGE 2
Operational, Maintenance and Sewerage Staff

Organisational Pathology: Communication Systems

The setting up of a Business Committee, with the same objectives as those outlined for Support staff, and the re-communication of the results of the Employee Opinion Survey to all staff through focus groups and meetings (objectives as for Support staff).

Organisational Pathology: Training and Development

The introduction of appraisals, or one-to-one reviews, for all staff with their line manager. These would be new to most staff and the Steering Group believed they would provide for increased feedback and a more solid basis for personal development.

360 degree appraisals (the use of colleague, supervisor and subordinate ratings in the appraisal process) were set up at one sewage treatment works site. This was implemented as a trial at one site to see whether there would be an impact on team working and foster increased understanding across different jobs and grades.

Management Training and Development programmes were strengthened, to allow managers to enhance their skills and expertise through training and assessment, e.g. National Vocational Qualifications. Again, this intervention had similar objectives to those given for Support Staff.

Mentors and buddies were provided for new production managers. Managers more senior to the employee would act as a mentor, and managers at the same level, but with more experience would act as buddies. The employee, mentor and buddy would decide amongst themselves the nature of the relationship, e.g. whether it would involve a formal meeting in work time, or a less formal get-together outside of work. The intervention was aimed at developing more able staff into management roles.

Organisational Pathology: Systems for the Auditing of Health and Safety Compliance

Auditing of the health and safety standards of contractors was introduced, including an overall audit by the Safety Manager, and 'Spot check' auditing, where the Safety Manager carried out a small, unannounced audit. This was designed to investigate and address employees' concern about the way contractors were working.

5. PHASE III: EVALUATION

5.1 PROCESS

Two evaluation questionnaires were designed to reflect the differences in the work done, and the problems reported, by office staff and manual workers. The evaluation questionnaires contained three sections: an abridged version of the Work Environment Survey, the battery of health measures, and an intervention inventory. These questionnaires were agreed by the Steering Group in September 1998. The questionnaires for Operational, Maintenance and Sewerage staff were distributed to Managers by the Occupational Health Medical Adviser in November 1998. Managers were then asked to distribute the questionnaires to their teams, and to return them either directly to Nottingham or to Occupational Health via prepaid envelopes. The Personnel Department at one of the sewage treatment sites distributed the questionnaires to Support staff, who were asked to return them to Nottingham also via prepaid envelopes. A series of interviews was conducted with a sample of staff from both groups in order to gather qualitative data on the impact of the interventions. This information was used to clarify and support the results of the evaluation.

The overall response rate for Support staff was 74% (59 questionnaires returned) and 33% for Operational, Maintenance and Sewerage staff (115 returned). These represented an increase in response rate for both groups compared with the original risk assessment. Respondents to the evaluation were similar to those employees who completed the original risk assessment questionnaires in terms of their age, gender, and length of service.

5.2 RESULTS

5.2.1 Support Staff

Differences Between 1997 and 1998

Support staff reported feeling slightly more 'worn out' and 'tense' in 1998 than at the time of the original risk assessment. The percentage of staff reporting work-related musculoskeletal pain remained stable, as did the proportion wishing to leave the company. Absence was stable. However, job satisfaction had decreased markedly.

There were some headline changes in the expert judgements of staff on their working conditions. Compared to the original risk assessment survey, 16% fewer staff reported that time pressures were problematic. 11% fewer staff reported problems with communication with senior management. There was also a 22 % drop in the number reporting that customers knew little about what Support staff actually did.

However, not all of the changes were positive. 22% more staff reported that job security was inadequate, and 23% more staff reported that participation in strategic decisions was problematic.

Organisational Penetration and Impact of the Interventions

Communication Systems
Nearly all Support staff were aware of the communication about the results of the Employee Opinion Survey, but 88% felt that it had not had any effects on their working conditions. Similarly, awareness of the Business Committee was low.

Training & Development
61% of the group reported that they had been involved in or affected by One-to-One Reviews, and 48% of these felt that it had made their conditions at work better. These appeared to have been well received. Those staff who were involved in or affected by the One-to-One Reviews were less likely to want to leave the Company than those people who were not involved in the Reviews. However, it was reported that as a result of many employees changing jobs within the company, not all employees had received a one-to-one review over the intervention period:

> *"One-to-one reviews have not happened for two years - I've changed jobs a lot"*

69% of managers reported that they had been involved in 'Management Training and Development', but only a handful of these felt that it had made their conditions at work better. However, there was a perception from those employees interviewed during the evaluation that Management Training had positive effects for the staff:

> *"The way that managers deal with their staff is much better now, since they went on training courses"*

Demands of Meetings
Only 30% of the group were aware of the new Meetings Etiquette, with only a fifth reporting that their work had improved as a result. This intervention appeared to have little impact, perhaps because of such low awareness levels.

Home – work Interface
A positive result was found for the increased availability of laptops. 75% of the group were aware of increased opportunities to work from home because of the increased availability of laptops. 51% of these reported that the change had improved their work. Those staff who were involved in or affected by the increased opportunity to work from home were less likely to report that they were exposed to the risks associated with VDU work. Additionally, they were more likely to be satisfied with the protection from those risks. Those staff who were involved in, or affected by, this intervention were also less likely to report experiencing work-related musculoskeletal pain.

5.2.2 Operational, Maintenance and Sewerage Staff

Differences Between 1997 and 1998

The health profile at evaluation revealed some mixed results. Compared to the risk assessment data, more staff reported experiencing work-related musculoskeletal pain. A greater number intended to leave their job if an opportunity arose elsewhere. Self-reported sickness absence had also increased slightly, as had the number reporting overall dissatisfaction with their job. In contrast, there was a drop in 'worn out' scores, and 'tense' scores remained steady (Figure 1 - below).

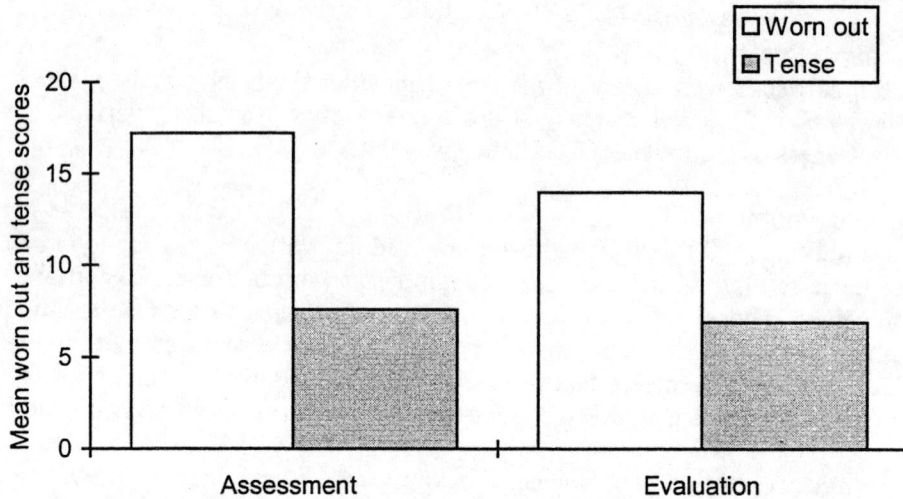

Figure 1: 'Worn out' and 'tense' scores: Operational, maintenance and sewerage staff

Compared to the risk assessment results, 23% fewer staff reported that there was a lack of encouragement to attend training courses. There was a slight drop in the proportion of employees reporting that time pressures and appreciation of the team's efforts by management were problematic.

Unfortunately, a greater proportion of staff reported problems with contractors not following health and safety requirements. There was also a slight increase in the number of staff reporting problems with performance monitoring.

Given the geographical spread of the this group of employees and varied nature of their day-to-day tasks, there was a clear need to look behind these data to identify the impact of specific interventions.

Organisational Penetration and Impact of the Interventions

Communication Systems
78% of the group reported that they were aware of the communication about the results from the Employee Opinion Survey, but only 12% of them felt it had made their conditions at work better. Although the staff interviewed during the evaluation reported that they appreciated being informed of the results, there was a perception that their comments would not be acted upon:

> *"We sat down with the senior manager - everybody on site - and could ask questions. But we didn't feel as if too much was acted upon - it was more a meeting where we were told what was happening rather than being given the opportunity to change things"*

Those staff who knew about, were involved in, or affected by the Business Committee (a small proportion of the group) were less likely to report problems with communication with senior management than those who did not know about this intervention. It was reported during the evaluation interviews that this intervention was successful in communicating matters occurring within the organisation to staff:

146

"Through the newsletter from the Business Committee, you get to hear more of things going on"

However, it was also reported during the evaluation interviews that more still needed to be done to address poor communication:

"We get inconsistent messages from management, with hidden meanings. From our immediate manager, we are promised much but they don't deliver"

Training & Development

40% of managers reported that they had been involved in, or affected by, the introduction of mentors. A quarter indicated their work was better as a result. 40% of the group reported that they had been involved in or affected by the introduction of One-to-One Reviews. Again, a quarter of these reported that the change had made their conditions at work better. However, it was also reported during the evaluation interviews that many employees disliked the one-to-one reviews because of the performance related pay component:

"It [the pay awards] is based upon personalities and how well you get on with your team leader.... It's not based on your performance"

Those staff who were involved in or affected by the One-to-One Reviews were less likely to report problems with performance monitoring than those staff not involved in or affected by the intervention. The one-to-one reviews appeared to be effective in giving staff the opportunity to express their opinions:

"If you do get a one-to-one, it gives you the chance to say how you feel"

"The one-to-one reviews are pretty good - your line manager will listen to what you have to say...you can get things off your chest, grievances, if your manager has anything to say to you, what you both expect of each other...they're usually willing to listen"

Similar results emerged for those staff who were involved in, or affected by 360 degree appraisals. These employees were also less likely to report problems with the way performance was monitored than those staff not involved in, or affected by, this intervention.

Systems for the Auditing of Health and Safety Compliance

30% of the group reported that they knew about, had been involved in, or affected by the auditing of health and safety standards of contractors by the Safety Manager. Few (20%) of these staff indicated that they felt that it had made their conditions at work better. Those staff who reported that they knew about, were involved in, or affected by the 'spot check' auditing were less likely to report being 'worn out' than those staff who did not know about the intervention. It was reported during the evaluation interviews that contractors' health and safety standards were variable, and depended on the particular sewerage treatment site at which they were working.

6. LEARNING POINTS

6.1 CO-OPERATION

The co-operation of senior management is vital to the success of such projects. In this case study, senior management were clearly aware of the need for a risk assessment for work stress, and were fully supportive of the project.

6.2 PRACTICALITIES

Familiarisation with employees' working conditions can be time consuming, particularly where the staff are widely dispersed geographically. This needs to be considered in the overall planning of the project. Sometimes compromises will need to be made. In this case study, it proved possible to visit all sites, but interviews were only conducted at a representative sample of those sites.

6.3 COMMUNICATION

It is important to ensure that lines of communication work well. At the beginning of this case study, potential interviewees were not always informed in advance of the date and time when they would be required. Employee representatives on the Steering Group helped to correct this problem by identifying more effective communication channels which were used in the later stages of the project.

6.4 DISTRIBUTION OF QUESTIONNAIRES

Measures should be taken to ensure that questionnaires are received by the intended respondents by making the distribution as direct as possible. In this case, distribution of questionnaires to employees' homes was affected by Personnel's records of employees' home addresses not being up-to-date. The distribution strategy was altered to address this problem. Response rates should be carefully monitored. Wherever possible, distribution and completion of questionnaires during work time is preferable. This also indicates management commitment to the project.

6.5 ORGANISATIONAL CHANGE

Changes occurring separately to, and outside the remit and control of the project can affect the design and implementation of interventions. During the time of the interventions, decisions were pending on a number of major changes (e.g. staffing levels).This was further confounded by low attendance by employee representatives at Steering Group meetings. The Steering Group usually consisted of managerial staff, and this may also have affected the design of the interventions. The Steering Group's chosen strategy was to design and implement a small number of interventions that could be quickly put in place, even during a period of uncertainty. As a consequence, some of the organisational pathologies and likely risk factors were not tackled. It was decided that the risk reduction activities had to work within boundaries dictated by the prevailing organisational situation. The results from the risk assessment were largely used to inform ongoing and future change programmes. However, opportunities to be creative in intervention design may still be available even when interventions have to 'ride on the back of' other planned organisational change.

6.6 FEEDBACK

Feedback of the results from both the risk assessment and evaluation to those employees involved in the project is essential. In this case study, results from previous employee surveys (e.g. previous opinion surveys) had not always been accompanied by feedback to staff. In such circumstances, feedback of the risk assessment and evaluation results represents an intervention in itself. Feedback was provided in this project and well received.

CASE STUDY 5

RAILWAY STATION SUPERVISORS

1. SUMMARY

This case study was carried out among Station Supervisors: shift work staff who managed the day-to-day running of railway stations on one of Britain's rail networks. 160 Supervisors were involved in the study, which was carried out over a period of just over two years. Together they were responsible for nearly 30 stations covering a wide geographical area. At the time of the study, the railway company was entering a period of uncertainty over its future structure.

1.1 PHASE I: RISK ASSESSMENT

The Station Supervisors reported 'worn out' and 'tense' scores that were higher than comparative norms. Many wanted to leave the company and job satisfaction was low. Absence levels were high, with a large proportion reporting work-related musculoskeletal pain. Many staff reported poor quality of sleep and low levels of exercise as well as irregular eating patterns. The risk assessment provided evidence of the existence of a number of stressors and likely risk factors (aspects of work associated with problems identified in the health profile). These were:

- Poor relationships with management, and a perceived lack of praise and recognition

- A need to spend much time juggling tasks of equal importance

- A lack of opportunities to use skills and develop a career

- The effect of shift work on family and leisure activities

- A lack of opportunities to take breaks

- Poor absence control procedures

- A lack of involvement in, and consultation about, decisions affecting the job (both in terms of day-to-day decision making and consultation about far-reaching changes)

- Inadequate staffing levels

- Intimidation from the public and, at times, other staff

1.2 PHASE II: TRANSLATION AND RISK REDUCTION

Through a series of meetings with the project Steering Group, and subsequently with Station Supervisors, that explored the underlying problems, a specific plan of action was designed. Many of the difficulties were believed to relate to communication problems within the company and a lack of trust. The interventions were:

- Action planning groups to address issues of communication and those of roles and responsibilities

- Team get-togethers, advance briefings, de-briefings, written communication briefings, and a Station Supervisor presence at senior management meetings

- A new communication link between train operations and station staff

- Competence based workshops to facilitate career progression

- Improved administration procedures for acknowledging and tracking correspondence

- Communication, clarification and expansion of roles and responsibilities

- An anti-intimidation poster campaign, and enhanced training for dealing with physical and verbal assault

1.3 PHASE III: EVALUATION

While the interventions were being introduced, the organisation entered a period of great uncertainty which was accompanied by industrial unrest. This difficult industrial climate, combined with the geographical spread of Station Supervisors and the company's long standing problems, inevitably meant that the impact of the interventions was reduced. The key findings were:

- Moderate, and sometimes low, awareness of the interventions

- Mixed, but generally positive, reactions to interventions from those staff who were aware of them

- Evidence that those Supervisors who were affected by the interventions viewed their work more positively

- Evidence of more positive well-being among those Supervisors who were involved in at least some of the interventions

Given the large number of stressors and likely risk factors identified in the risk assessment, the demands of the work carried out by Station Supervisors, and the industrial unrest within the organisation throughout the project, it was encouraging to find some positive results emerging from the evaluation. There was evidence to suggest that some of these positive results appeared to be linked to an awareness of, or involvement in, some of the interventions.

2. BACKGROUND

The company involved in the project provides a railway service for one of the UK's major cities. This project focused on one route containing a large number of stations, staffed by approximately 140 Station Supervisors working on a three-shift system. The stations on the periphery of the line are lightly staffed, and the Station Supervisor could be the only person working at the station. Other busier stations had two or three Supervisors, who managed 30 - 40 other station staff. Duties for Station Supervisors were extensive and varied. The job could involve any type of work in the station. This might include operating ticket barriers, advising passengers, issuing penalty fares, making announcements, all aspects of station staff management, selling tickets, monitoring CCTV, monitoring health and safety, dealing with crowd control, liaising with the ticket office and maintaining the necessary paperwork. The Supervisor was also the hub of communication for the station, and other staff would come to them for advice or to report problems. The Supervisor would also pass on information to the public regarding delays or cancellations to trains.

The Supervisors' job could be a busy one. It involved a number of different roles, and in the busier stations work could be extremely pressured. In some of the quieter stations Supervisors worked alone, which could create problems when difficulties arose, or when the station was unusually busy. Being at the 'centre' of the running of station operations, Supervisors were subject to the demands of senior management, the public and their own station staff. Communication was difficult across the wide geographical area covered by the line. In the wider context, the company had a recent history of troubled industrial relations. Investment within the railway network had been limited for some time.

Stations were grouped together for management purposes. Each group of 5-6 stations was managed by a Duty Station Manager (DSM) who was charged with overseeing the running of stations by the Station Supervisors. This was a relatively new post which had been created, among other things, to support health and safety processes and to provide a link between the stations and senior management. At the beginning of the project, senior management expressed some concern that relations between Supervisors and DSMs were not as good as they could have been.

Employee representatives (both Union representatives and Station Supervisors) and management made up the core of the Steering Group. Others involved included representatives from Occupational Health and Personnel. With the project being carried out against a backdrop of change and strained industrial relations, input from the Steering Group was especially crucial and always lively.

3. PHASE I: RISK ASSESSMENT

3.1 PROCESS

A prolonged period of Familiarisation was carried out, and included a number of presentations on the aims and objectives of the project were targeted at building trust and setting expectations. Workplace visits and the inspection of organisational data (particularly job descriptions, results of previous staff surveys, and performance and workload statistics) provided much useful information. 20 Work Analysis Interviews were carried out with Station Supervisors from all parts of the route and all types of stations. Ten Management Systems Audit Interviews were also conducted at this time. Using information from the interviews, organisational documentation, stakeholder interviews, and walkthrough observations, the Work Environment Survey was tailored to the needs and context of the Station Supervisors. Despite differences in the type of work carried out at different types of stations, a sufficient number of common issues existed to allow for the design of a single assessment questionnaire that would provide 'good enough' data. The project team worked with employee and management representatives to ensure the questionnaire was relevant, comprehensive and user-friendly. The input of the Steering Group was especially useful when considering a number of sensitive issues that were related to recent problems within the company. The risk assessment questionnaire was agreed and then distributed in June 1996. 70% (112) of the questionnaires were returned: this was received well by the Steering Group. A much lower return had been expected due to the industrial relations problems.

3.2 RESULTS

The health profile of the group was assessed by comparing the results from Station Supervisors to national norms, for people involved in broadly similar work. Station Supervisors reported being more 'worn out' and 'tense' than the national average. A high percentage of them (66%) reported work-related musculoskeletal pain. Absence levels were relatively high at 12 days per year. Few staff (24%) were satisfied with their job, with around half wishing to leave their job. However, actual turnover was low. Staff also reported poor quality sleep, low levels of exercise, and irregular eating patterns.

There was strong agreement among the Supervisors about the problems they were facing, and very many of these problems proved to be likely risk factors. By considering both the number of Supervisors reporting each problem and the strength with which each was associated with poor health, a 'manageable' number of issues emerged. Through discussion with the Steering Group, it became clear that there was a list of likely risk factors which should be addressed by interventions:

- Inadequate communication with, and support from, management

- Lack of praise and recognition of effort

- Lack of involvement in and consultation about decisions affecting the job (e.g. buying and maintaining station equipment and a host of related issues)

- Problems in balancing demands from the public with other job demands (e.g. paperwork)

- Inadequate control over who did what in the stations (i.e. staff allocation)

- Inadequate career prospects and career development structures

- Lack of time for training and too few opportunities to use their full range of skills

- Rigidity of working hours and the effect of shift work on family and leisure activities

- Few chances to take breaks

- Absence control procedures

- Inadequate staffing

- Intimidation by the public and other staff

4. PHASE II: TRANSLATION AND RISK REDUCTION

During September 1996, the results from the risk assessment were fed back to the project Steering Group, and separately to the Station Supervisors. As an initial response, the Steering Group members indicated that they had expected communication, trust and various workload issues to be the most significant problems. A one page summary of findings was sent to all the Supervisors involved.

From initial discussions it appeared that a number of the problems identified were complex and potentially difficult to tackle. The organisation was large and, being at the hub station operations, the actions of any number of people could impact on the work of the Station Supervisor. In addition to this, staff were working in a rather uncertain and turbulent organisational climate. However, in order to formulate an action plan, a series of Steering Group meetings were planned.

Initial discussions focused on identifying specific actions to tackle specific problems. However, little headway was made as discussions became bogged down in detail. To break this 'log jam', Steering Group meetings were facilitated to reduce the list of problems. To achieve this, the project team re-focused the debate in order to identify a smaller number of underlying issues (e.g. a lack of a clear definition of roles and responsibilities underlying lack of trust, workload and communication issues). A number of Station Supervisors were interviewed again at this stage to gather further information. This information was then introduced into the Steering Group discussions. As a result, the Steering Group took a 'broader' view of the issues, and began to draw out an organisational pathology which appeared to underlie a number of risk factors and stressors. These 'clusters' of issues related to: roles and responsibilities, communication problems and their implications for workload, staff development, and intimidation and assault. Using this pathology, the Steering Group began to suggest innovative solutions. Most of the interventions reported here were the direct result of the discussions within the Steering Group. Where particularly difficult issues were identified, or when the Steering Group was unsure as to the exact nature of the problem, interventions were designed that would involve the Station Supervisors in the development of possible solutions.

After some initial difficulties, the intervention design was successful. However, implementation of some of the interventions required the approval of, and support from, parties external to the Steering Group. At times this was a slow process in the prevailing climate of industrial unrest and uncertainty. Relationships between the unions and management had to be carefully managed, since the support and ideas of both parties was essential during implementation. The final package of interventions is detailed on the following page.

INTERVENTION PACKAGE
Station Supervisors

Organisational Pathology: Roles & Responsibilities

A number of communication and roles and responsibilities action planning meetings were set up. Each meeting lasted 4-5 hours and was designed and facilitated by the project team. These were designed to give staff the opportunity to give more detailed information about the strengths and weaknesses of current communication systems, and job role definitions. Staff were challenged to devise practical solutions to problems. This intervention was also a way of increasing employee involvement and provided information for the design of subsequent interventions.

Job and responsibility enlargement was introduced through communications about Station Supervisors' responsibilities to report faulty station equipment, check the quality of work done by contractors, and be involved in the discipline of staff. Job descriptions were also made available to staff to support this process.

A further intervention was the clarification of responsibilities of Duty Station Managers. It was reported in both the risk assessment questionnaire, and subsequent action planning meetings that some of the problems experienced by Station Supervisors had their root in misunderstandings or breakdowns in communication between Station Supervisors and Duty Station Managers (DSMs). To address such problems, a number of measures were taken including: the clarification of the DSMs' responsibilities regarding managing the staffing of stations, reminding DSMs about their responsibility to keep staff informed of their whereabouts, and emphasising the need for DSMs to give Station Supervisors 7 days' advance notice of training sessions. Some of the changes were devised during the action planning meetings.

Organisational Pathology: Communication Problems with Implications for Workload

A number of measures to improve communication with immediate and senior management including team get-togethers, advance briefings on known changes, written communication briefings, de-briefing sessions after major events, and representation at senior management meetings.

A new Line Information Assistant was appointed to work at the railway communication centre. The role of this member of staff was to pass information relevant to the running of trains along the line to Station Supervisors on that line. This was designed to help Supervisors anticipate and plan for problems, while keeping the public better informed.

Tighter auditing of correspondence procedures was also implemented. Station Supervisors reported that written queries were 'lost' in the system, and they were often unsure whether letters or memos they sent to their managers were receiving attention. To help remedy this problem, a procedure was introduced whereby all correspondence sent to immediate managers was to be acknowledged within one day of receipt.

Organisational Pathology: Staff Development

Competence based workshops were designed to help able Station Supervisors progress within the company. These provided information about what was required from staff in order to achieve the company's criteria for promotion. The goal of this intervention was to help promising staff present themselves more effectively during the promotions procedure (e.g. in completing application forms).

INTERVENTION PACKAGE (continued)

Station Supervisors
Organisational Pathology: Assault and Intimidation A Poster campaign in mess-rooms designed to increase staff awareness of the company's supportive policy with regard to assault and intimidation by the public. The campaign was supported by a programme of specialised training designed to help staff deal with situations involving assault or threatening behaviour.

5. PHASE III: EVALUATION

5.1 METHOD

A second questionnaire-based survey was central to the evaluation strategy and provided data that could be directly compared with those gathered during the risk assessment phase. Other methods, those such as stakeholder interviews, and the examination of organisational documentation, provided additional information. The evaluation was carried out in November 1998.

As with the risk assessment, the central part of the evaluation involved gathering employee expert judgements on the adequacy of aspects of their work (the Work Environment Survey). Stakeholder interviews and company documentation were used to support the development of an intervention inventory, which was added to a shortened version of the risk assessment survey. The evaluation survey focused on identifying progress on the likely risk factors and stressors identified in the risk assessment phase. The Steering Group checked and agreed the survey. 62 (39%) of the questionnaires were returned. It was thought that the poor industrial relations climate and widespread uncertainty about the organisation's future had contributed to the lower return rate. However, in terms of average age, length of service, gender, and the stations worked at, those completing the questionnaire in 1998 formed a very similar group to those who contributed to the risk assessment in 1996.

5.2 RESULTS

Differences Between 1996 and 1998

There were a number of changes in staff perceptions of their work. The volatile organisational climate over the period of the interventions made the data somewhat difficult to interpret. For example, exposure to some of the original stressors appeared to have worsened. Compared to 1996, more staff reported problems with the allocation of commendations (memos and notes on personnel files that acknowledged exceptional performance), the maintenance of buildings, and consultation in decisions regarding the purchasing and maintenance of equipment. Many of the original problems persisted.

However, despite the turbulent background, a number of improvements were noted. A smaller proportion of Supervisors rated career development as a problem. Shift length was seen as a problem by a slightly smaller proportion of staff in 1998 than in 1996. In 1996, over 70% of the Supervisors reported that lack of opportunities to take breaks was a problem. This figure had reduced to 40% in 1998. A far greater proportion of Supervisors reported that their shift patterns were predictable, with 20% fewer reporting this area of their work as a problem. In the 'headline' figures on employee health, there was little overall difference from 1996 except for a decreased incidence of musculoskeletal pain, and a slight reduction in report of being 'worn out'.

As has already been mentioned, the Supervisors were spread over a wide geographical area, worked within a fairly loose organisational structure, and were faced with unpredictable and varied demands. The organisational climate was turbulent. Therefore, it was possible that some interventions were either inconsistently applied, went unnoticed, or made less difference than they should have done. Such inconsistencies may have been particularly relevant for staff at the sharp end of the organisation's problems. In order to tease out the impact of interventions, Supervisors were asked whether they had been aware of, involved in, or effected by the interventions (a measure was taken of the organisational penetration of the interventions using an intervention inventory).

Organisational Penetration and Impact of the Interventions

Prior to the evaluation, discussions with key stakeholders indicated that interventions had been inconsistently implemented, and it was anticipated that awareness of some interventions would be low. Therefore, in order to assess the impact of the interventions, it was particularly important to identify Supervisors who were aware of the changes, and those who believed the change had improved their work. Results indicated that awareness of the interventions was indeed 'patchy' across stations. Within this patchy pattern of awareness, groups of staff receiving the intervention could be isolated from, and compared to, groups who had not. From this it became apparent that many Supervisors who were aware of, or involved in, many of the interventions indicated that the changes had made a difference to their work.

Roles & Responsibilities

Though only 38% of supervisors were aware of the action planning meetings, most were aware of job and responsibility enlargement through fault reporting and the checking of contractor work (71% and 88% respectively). Since relatively few staff were involved in the action planning meetings through the intervention period, few Supervisors reported that their work had improved as a result. However, responsibility enlargement through the checking of contractors' work and fault reporting were the most positively received of interventions. Over a third of those who were aware of them, and the majority of those who had been affected by them, said that their job had improved as a result.

Staff who were aware of the enlargement of responsibility through fault reporting indicated feeling less 'worn out' and 'tense', and were less likely to report musculoskeletal pain, than those staff who were not aware of the change. Awareness of this intervention was also linked to positive evaluations of a number of aspects of the job including satisfactory control over the allocation of work, acceptable workload, reasonable time pressures and a lower incidence of harassment. Many Supervisors also indicated that the intervention had improved their job. These Supervisors were less likely to be dissatisfied with their job. The perception that the job had improved through the intervention was accompanied by positive evaluations of consultation, senior management communication and support, and feedback from line management.

As with the fault reporting system, staff who were aware of the communication regarding the inspection of contractor sites were less likely to report high 'worn out' or 'tense' scores, than those who were not aware of the change. The change also appeared to be linked to satisfaction with opportunities available to use job-related skills. As was expected, those staff who thought the intervention had improved their work were more likely to indicate that they were satisfied with consultation about station equipment. Positive evaluations of the intervention were also linked to favourable evaluations of communication with senior management, recognition of effort, and feedback from line management. Staff reacting positively were less likely to want to leave the company, or be dissatisfied with their job.

40% were aware of the renewed availability of job descriptions. Those staff who were aware of this intervention were less likely to be dissatisfied with opportunities to use their skills, the status of their work, their workload, and recognition of their efforts.

Fewer staff (38%) were aware that staff discipline had become a personal development issue. Taking more responsibility for staff discipline was something that Supervisors could now discuss at appraisals, and have added to their job descriptions if appropriate. Supervisors who were aware that taking more responsibility for staff discipline was something that could be discussed and addressed at appraisals tended to view management positively. They were less likely to be dissatisfied with support from senior management and informal feedback from their immediate manager. They were also less likely to report harassment than Supervisors who were not aware of the change.

The majority of Supervisors (73%) reported being aware of the new procedures in place to help them locate their immediate manage, although only a fifth reported their job had improved as a result. There was evidence to suggest that an awareness of this intervention was linked to a number of positive findings. Supervisors who were aware of the intervention were less likely to be dissatisfied with the level of protection from the risks in their job, their workload, time pressures, break-taking opportunities and control over the allocation of tasks. They were also less likely to be dissatisfied with their job overall than those who were not aware that these changes had occurred.

A significant proportion (37% and 40% respectively) of Supervisors were aware of the clarification of their immediate manager's responsibilities for managing the staffing of stations, and providing 7 days' notice for training. Supervisors who were aware of reminders to immediate managers about their responsibility for ensuring station staffing levels were less likely to be dissatisfied with a number of workload issues including balancing priorities, time pressures and control over the distribution of work. The provision of time for training, support from senior management, status of their job and protection from the workplace also tended to be viewed positively by the group who were aware.

Organisational Pathology: Communication Problems with Implications for Workload
The reaction to the measures taken to improve communication was mixed. 55% were aware of or had been involved in written communications briefings, though slightly fewer (35%) were aware of either advance briefings on known changes or de-briefings after major events (41%). 45% were aware of team 'get-togethers'. Involvement in team 'get-togethers' appeared to be linked to a number of health related measures. Those who had been involved were less likely to report high levels of absence, musculoskeletal pain, or job dissatisfaction. Perhaps related to this was the finding that Supervisors who reported that get-togethers had improved their work were the least likely to report harassment and intimidation. In terms of evaluating their work, those involved in the intervention were less likely to report that opportunities to use their skills and informal feedback from their manager were inadequate. Favourable reactions to the intervention were associated with positive findings on a number of communication and management support issues including the communication of company policy, involvement in (and control over) decisions, and support from senior management. Adequate recognition of effort was also more likely to be reported by those who indicated that the get-togethers had improved their job.

Awareness of Supervisor representation at senior management meetings was extremely low (only 20%). One fifth of those who were aware of team get-togethers and de-briefings reported that their work had improved as a result, but this represented a high success rate for those who had been *actively involved* in these events. Success rates were far lower for representation at management meetings and written communication briefings. However, compared to staff who were not aware of them, staff who were aware of advance briefings on known events reported lower 'worn out' scores and were less likely to report high levels of absence, or dissatisfaction with their job. Awareness of these briefings was linked to satisfaction with break-taking arrangements, levels of participation, recognition, consultation and communication.

Involvement in de-briefing sessions with line managers was linked to satisfaction with the level of participation and consultation in decisions and communication with immediate and senior management. Those who were affected by this intervention were less likely to report inadequate protection against risks to health and safety, or dissatisfaction with their job overall. Similar results were found for those who indicated that the intervention had improved their work.

Encouragingly, most Supervisors (67%) knew about the appointment of the Line Information Assistant (LIA), with over a third of those indicating that this had improved their work. It was anticipated that this intervention would have most impact on certain parts of the line affected by the sudden re-routing of trains. It appeared that the introduction of the Line Information Assistant was associated with improved opportunities for Supervisors to exercise their abilities. Station Supervisors who were aware of the LIA were less likely to be dissatisfied with opportunities to use their skills. These Supervisors were also less likely to report harassment, musculoskeletal pain, and overall job dissatisfaction than those who were not aware of the LIA. The intervention also seemed to be associated with satisfactory levels of communication with management. Those staff who said their job had been improved by the introduction of the LIA were less likely to be dissatisfied with levels of communication with senior management, and the amount of informal feedback from their manager.

Fewer than one in three (32%) were aware of the new auditing procedures in place to track correspondence, with very few (12%) of these saying their work was better as a result. Perhaps as a results of these findings, analysis suggested that the impact of this intervention on stressors and risk factors was minimal.

Organisational Pathology: Staff Development

48% of the Supervisors were aware of the competence based workshops. Given the relatively low levels of participation in them (due to the limited availability of the workshops in the early stages of the intervention), the finding that one fifth of those aware of them believed their work was better as a result was relatively encouraging. However, at the time of evaluation, too few staff had been involved in the intervention to allow for the evaluation of the impact of the workshops on concerns about training and development.

Organisational Pathology: Assault and Intimidation

Most Supervisors (80%) were aware of the poster campaign and specialised training for dealing with assaults (68%). Around one fifth of the Supervisors said that their work had improved as a result of these interventions. Although this appears to be a modest response, for interventions requiring only staff awareness such as a poster campaign these results are acceptable. There was evidence to suggest that those staff who were aware of the poster campaign were less likely to report high levels of absence, job dissatisfaction, or intimidation than those who were not aware of the poster campaign. Those staff who thought the campaign had improved their work were more likely to believe that the protection offered from the risks inherent in their job was adequate. They also reported fewer and less frequent symptoms relating to tension and anxiety than those who said their job had not improved as a result.

The training for dealing with assaults had a lengthy 'roll out' period, that began during the latter part of the intervention. Consequently, few Supervisors had been offered the training at the time of the evaluation. The resultant low level of involvement in the training accounted for the small proportion of staff reporting that it had improved their job. The organisation had plans to offer the training to all Supervisors in the future. At the time of writing, too few staff were appropriately involved to enable the formation of comparison groups to allow for the analysis of the impact of this intervention.

One other intervention was positively received: the routine issuing of station keys to new members of staff. 42% were aware of it, and a third of those who were aware of it reported that the intervention had made their work better.

Commentary
Given the large number of stressors and likely risk factors identified in the risk assessment, the demands of the work carried out by Station Supervisors, and the industrial unrest within the organisation throughout the project, it was encouraging to find some positive results emerging from the evaluation. There was evidence to suggest that some of these positive results were linked to an awareness of, or involvement in, some of the interventions.

6. LEARNING POINTS

6.1 COMMUNICATION

Communication can be difficult within large organisations, or when those involved in the risk assessment are spread over a wide geographical area. This situation can be exacerbated when a number of different groups have a stake in the project (e.g. personnel, trade unions, management, etc.). In this project, such problems were managed through regular and frequent Steering Group meetings at key points within the project. News about the project was included in Supervisors' 'must read' circulars. The project team were 'on-site' during both periods of questionnaire completion to raise the profile of the project and to encourage employees to respond. Assessment and intervention have a much greater chance of success when communication problems are effectively managed.

6.2 ORGANISATIONAL CLIMATE

Interventions rarely take place during a period of stability in any organisation. It is a fact of life that organisations and work change to meet business needs. During the course of this project industrial relations were strained because of plans announced about the long-term future of the organisation. Clearly, such issues have implications for the risk assessment and the impact of interventions. The risk assessment needs to be a robust enough procedure to survive, and work within, such circumstances. At a practical level, measures were taken to ensure that issues surrounding the industrial action were not discussed at Steering Group meetings. These meetings were 'ring fenced' against industrial relations issues. Data collection was not carried out during times of particular unrest. The project was marketed as something distinct from the issues surrounding the industrial dispute.

6.3 DEVELOPING TRUST

Developing trust can be difficult where there is, for whatever reasons, discontent or a history of troubled industrial relations. Many employees may see a questionnaire that asks them to judge their work design and management issues as having a hidden agenda. Making unequivocal assurances about confidentiality and anonymity addresses this problem to a degree. It was made clear that the risk assessment was entirely concerned with the work system and its problems, and in no way targeted individuals. In practical terms, trust should be developed through open communication in the marketing of the project, the interventions and their results. Where possible, face-to-face communication was attempted so that employees could ask questions. This strategy gave the project a 'human face'. The project team spent much time travelling around the stations during both the risk assessment and evaluation phases, in an attempt to address concerns regarding the project. High profile stakeholder endorsement from both unions and management also helped. All written communications were signed by union, management, occupational health and personnel representatives. Enlisting people who were trusted and respected by employees helped to get staff 'on-board'.

6.4 'PICKING OUT' THE POSITIVES

Geography, long-standing communication problems and the industrial relations climate meant that the interventions did not reach as many people as they perhaps could have. The volatile climate may well have 'diluted' the impact of some of the interventions. This could lead to a conclusion that the interventions had not been effective. However, it was apparent that some people were more aware of the interventions than others. Encouragingly, employees who were aware of, and reacted positively to, the interventions tended to be less likely to be dissatisfied with their work and more likely to report favourable scores on the health measures.

6.5 DESIGNING INTERVENTIONS

Designing the interventions can be one of the most difficult and time consuming parts of the project. This process requires a combination of original thought, stakeholder commitment and a willingness to examine difficult issues. There were a large number of long-standing problems in the company. While management reported that some local interventions were in place to tackle many of the issues, these had largely been ineffective. Faced with a long list of likely risk factors, Steering Group discussions became bogged down in detail. However, through carefully facilitated discussions, a number of underlying problems (pathologies) were identified. The design of interventions was then aimed at addressing these underlying issues. Using these pathologies in the design of interventions and their implementation proved effective in breaking down barriers to progress. Arguably, interventions devised in this way were the most effective in this organisation.

6.6 PRIORITISING PROBLEMS

When faced with a long list of likely risk factors, it can be difficult to know where to start planning interventions. To identify the priority issues, two pieces of information were considered: the number of workers who reported a particular problem with the work, and how likely it was that the problem was associated with poor health. This threw up seven or eight priority areas. This was further reduced by looking for the underlying causes of the problems (se 6.5 above). Sometimes it was possible to identify 'quick wins' for some of the issues. However, in order to maintain the momentum of the project, focusing on a manageable number of issues appeared to be an effective strategy.

6.7 SETTING EXPECTATIONS

Within this organisation, different stakeholders were expecting different outcomes from the project. Union representatives were expecting sweeping changes, while management were hoping that the project team would prescribe 'quick fix' interventions. There also appeared to be a debate between the parties over what was meant by 'reasonably practicable' in terms of interventions. It is important to take time to address these issues at the start of the project. In this company an early Steering Group meeting was devoted to 'walking-through' the project with the key stakeholders. This allowed them to see what was likely to happen at each stage. It was also important to inform the Steering Group that they would play an active role in the design of interventions, and that interventions may take time to work. It was pointed out to the Steering Group that rather than tackling every problem, it was preferable to secure commitment for a few key interventions. The project team made it clear that they were not prescribers of change: rather their role was to facilitate change driven by, and implemented from within, the organisation.

6.8 KEEPING EMPLOYEES INVOLVED

It is essential that people from within the assessment group have an influential role in all stages of the project. They will need time away from their job for meetings, and should be able to appoint a deputy if they are unavailable. Employee representatives should present the views and expertise of staff. They should also be comfortable liaising with management. In some cases union representatives may be ideal for this role. However, in this organisation the key union representatives were not Supervisors on the Line involved. In this case Station Supervisors were brought into the group regardless of union affiliation. Where unions play a key role in the employee-management relationship, their support for these projects should be sought. However, it is also crucial to include employee expertise in the Steering Group.

CASE STUDY 6

STORAGE, PACKAGING AND DISTRIBUTION CENTRE STAFF

1. SUMMARY

This case study was carried out among two groups of employees from a storage, packaging and distribution centre in the Midlands. The centre formed part of a large British engineering company. Packaging staff and Non-Packaging staff (mainly office and clerical staff) were involved in the project.

1.1 PHASE I: RISK ASSESSMENT

The risk assessment was carried out in November 1996. Packaging staff reported feeling more 'worn out' and 'tense' than comparable work groups, and reported higher levels of musculoskeletal pain, smoking, job dissatisfaction, and intention to leave. Non-Packaging staff felt less 'worn out' and 'tense' than similar work groups, but reported higher levels of job dissatisfaction, and many wanted to leave the company. The risk assessment identified different likely risks factors and other major stressors for each of the groups. These were targeted for intervention:

Packaging Staff

- Lack of recognition of effort and feedback on performance
- Lack of advance notice on urgent packing work
- Poor availability of medical staff
- Lack of equipment to help with packing jobs
- Problems with environmental conditions (e.g. variable temperatures, and poor air quality)
- Inadequate training and opportunities to develop skills
- Lack of communication between departments, and with senior and site management
- Harassment and intimidation from other staff

Non-Packaging Staff

- Lack of control over workload and participation in decisions
- Lack of recognition of efforts
- Senior management not appearing to know what the job involved
- Unclear job descriptions
- Lack of career development and prospects
- Lack of space
- Inadequate help from other staff
- Lack of communication and support from immediate and senior managers
- Lack of encouragement for sharing work problems
- Intimidation from other staff

1.2 PHASE II: TRANSLATION AND RISK REDUCTION

During the period of the assessment, the company merged with another large organisation. Feedback of the results from the risk assessment to the Steering Group was then used to inform the new management's programme of change. The major changes associated with the merger made it difficult for management to introduce interventions solely as a direct response to the risk assessment. The project team worked closely with site management to monitor the changes that were relevant to the risk assessment. These are detailed below:

> - Appointment of a Capacity Planner and Original Equipment Service Planner, combined with the monitoring of customer receipts against forecasts – all designed to improve planning and resource management
>
> - Introduction of appraisals at all levels
>
> - Restructuring of daily briefings, supported by quarterly briefings from senior managers
>
> - Introduction of training schedules for each employee and related problem solving events
>
> - Movement of some packaging staff into a more 'environmentally friendly' area
>
> - A number of interventions targeted at improved 'housekeeping'
>
> - 'Traditional' risk assessments carried out for every area and activity
>
> - Introduction of framed display posters and handouts detailing the company's goals and objectives
>
> - Job enlargement for many packing staff

1.3 PHASE III: EVALUATION

Due to factors related to the merger including uncertainty over the immediate future of the whole operation, it was not possible to directly question staff about the impact of the interventions. However, the expert judgements of key stakeholders were gathered. The evaluation was carried out in October 1998, and involved a series of one-to-one confidential interviews with key stakeholders. Those interviewed indicated that many of the interventions represented improvements to their working conditions.

2. BACKGROUND

The storage, packaging and distribution centre involved in this project is based in the Midlands. It is part of large British engineering organisation involved in the manufacturing and distribution of motor vehicle components. The centre was built in 1940, originally as an aircraft base, but was taken over by the organisation in 1964 and converted into a distribution centre. Manufactured products are delivered from the organisation's factories and other world-wide suppliers to the distribution centre for packaging into a saleable condition. These products are then stored in the site's warehouse until they are dispatched to locations throughout the world. At the time of the risk assessment, the site employed almost 650 staff across its packaging, storage and distribution functions. These staff were responsible for processing around 500-600 packaging orders, and dispatching around 700 pallets and 950 parcels of packed products per day.

The case study was carried out among two groups of employees from one area of the Packaging Centre (known as Warehouse No 5): Packaging staff and Non-Packaging staff. The Packaging staff did a number of different jobs. The majority were based within the Hand-pack and Machine-pack sections. Hand-pack dealt with orders that contained products which could not be dealt with by machines. The job generally involved putting medium sized mechanical components into boxes. Pallets containing the unpacked products and the appropriate number of boxes were left at the desks. Packing was generally carried out at a desk or table, but heavier items could be packed on the floor. At the start of the working day, employees took a card which indicated the products they had to pack and at which desk. Machine-pack carried out similar tasks but the actual packaging of products into boxes was done on machines of various sizes and types. Staff loaded and unloaded machines. The products and boxes were delivered to the machines on pallets. These sections were supported by the Receiving Deck, which contained a small number of staff who moved boxes into and out of storage (using cranes, forklifts etc.) and delivered them to the packaging staff.

The other group involved in the risk assessment, Non-Packaging staff, comprised of employees who worked in the offices that supported the packaging operation. These staff processed orders, provided a link to Head Office, and checked and labelled the packed products.

The project was initiated by the central Health and Safety Unit. However, the project was managed locally, by staff from the packaging site. The Steering Group, included the Warehouse Manager, staff and management from both sections, the site nurse, a trade union representative, personnel representatives, and senior management from the site.

3. PHASE I : RISK ASSESSMENT

3.1 PROCESS

Once it was agreed, the project was publicised through a series of mass meetings two weeks before it began. Familiarisation was extensive. Workplace observations were carried out over two days in conjunction with a series of 20 Work Analysis Interviews and eight Management Systems Audit interviews. The company kept extensive record detailing absence, turnover, health and safety, and workload (e.g. the number of pallets dispatched). These were examined as part of the Familiarisation stage. Although the work carried out by the two groups of staff was different, a number of common issues were raised in the Work Analysis Interviews. Furthermore, there were a number of similarities in the organisational terminology and language used by the two groups to describe their problems. Therefore, only one assessment instrument was designed. This included both the common issues and those unique to each group. The assessment instrument was agreed by the Steering Group in November 1996.

A communication memo was used to re-publicise the project and remind staff of the importance of the risk assessment survey. The survey was distributed to employees by their team leaders. The project team visited the site to explain how to complete the survey, and to collect completed questionnaires. However, only a low response rate was achieved. The project team then revisited the site to redistribute the questionnaires in person. The overall response rate was increased to 48%.

3.2 RESULTS

3.2.1 Packaging Staff

The health profile of the Packaging staff indicated that they felt more 'worn out' and 'tense', and reported higher levels of musculoskeletal pain (67 %), and smoking (amongst the men), than other groups of manual workers. Absence was moderate to low at 5 days per year although the organisation believed this was too high. Job satisfaction was low (53 % dissatisfied), and intention to leave was high. A number of were likely risk factors were associated with this health profile. There were also a number of other major stressors reported. Together, these were:

> - Lack of advance notice on urgent work
>
> - Lack of recognition of efforts
>
> - Lack of quality feedback from senior management about performance
>
> - Lack of availability of medical staff
>
> - Lack of equipment to help with packaging tasks
>
> - Poor environmental conditions (such as variable temperatures, and poor air quality)
>
> - Poor training, and a lack of opportunities to develop skills
>
> - Lack of communication between departments, sections, and with senior and site management
>
> - Harassment and intimidation

3.2.2 NON-PACKAGING STAFF

Compared with other samples of office-based staff, the Non-Packaging staff felt less 'worn out' and 'tense', and reported similar levels of smoking, consumption of alcohol and musculoskeletal disorders (37 % reporting work-related pain). However, job satisfaction was low (59 % dissatisfied), and intention to leave relatively high

A number of likely risk factor and associated problems were identified:

- Lack of control over workload and fluctuations in workload
- Lack of recognition of efforts
- Management not being aware of what the job involved
- Unclear job descriptions
- Lack of career development and prospects
- Inadequate work space
- Lack of help from other staff
- Lack of communication and support from immediate and senior managers
- Lack of opportunities to participate in decisions
- Lack of encouragement for sharing work problems
- Intimidation

4. PHASE II : TRANSLATION AND RISK REDUCTION

The results from the risk assessment were fed back to the Steering Group in May 1997, and were well received. However, during the risk assessment period, the organisation merged with a US company, resulting in significant changes to the management team on site. The new management team immediately embarked on a major change programme. This had a major impact on the project and the influence of the Steering Group.

The new management team indicated that a number of significant changes were likely to be implemented on site as a result of the merger. Therefore it became inappropriate and impractical for the Steering Group to design interventions solely using the results from the risk assessment. However, the new management team acknowledged the value of the risk assessment, and were keen for the results to be used to inform their change programme. A summary of the interventions that drew upon the risk assessment is presented below. Many were relevant to both groups of employees.

INTERVENTION PACKAGE
Packaging and Non-Packaging Staff

A 'Capacity Planner' and 'Original Equipment Service Planner' were appointed, and the monitoring of customer receipts against forecasts was introduced. These interventions were designed **to improve planning and resources** and to reduce the incidence of sudden, unexpected demands.

Appraisals were introduced at all levels to give staff more regular feedback, and more structured career and personal development opportunities. Training schedules were devised for each employee and events aimed at 'Continuous Improvement' took place. In these events, teams containing staff from all levels worked together to solve specific problems related to the running of the operation.

The **Hand-pack operation was moved** into a more environmentally friendly area, where there was less dust, and noise and more space.

A number of improvements were made to **housekeeping**. These changes included: the sealing and painting of floors, purchasing of vacuum cleaners for use by Packaging staff, training events to address cleanliness, the restructuring of the Housekeeping Review, and the introduction of a 'Dream Team' (two members of staff employed solely to maintain a clean environment). Risk assessments of the physical working environment were carried out for every area and activity, both to tackle perceived poor environmental conditions and reduce the incidence of musculoskeletal pain.

There was a re-structuring of the **daily team briefings**, and quarterly communications with site managers and director of logistics. These changes were designed to improve senior management communications. In addition, framed display posters displayed and 'handouts' were distributed containing information on the company's goals and objectives.

Within Machine-pack, **packing jobs were 'enlarged'**. Packaging staff were tasked with collating the goods and boxes they needed for each packaging job. To do this they were given 'pick notes' and access to storage areas. Before the intervention, the work in this area consisted of loading and monitoring the machines that packed products into boxes. This intervention was aimed at improving efficiency, reducing packaging times, and increasing the amount of variety and interest within the job.

---

5. PHASE III : EVALUATION

Just after the risk assessment, the merger between the British company and a US organisation resulted in a major programme of change on site. This included the out-sourcing of the storage operation in September 1998, changes to the packaging operations, and 130 voluntary redundancies between June 1997 and September 1997.

As indicated earlier, the management team and Steering Group felt that, in the light of this change programme, it would be inappropriate to carry out a further survey. However, they were willing for the project team to carry out an extensive series of one-to-one confidential interviews with managers and key stakeholders from the site. These interviews took place in October 1998, together with an observation of the new workplaces. The interviews were audio taped with the permission of each interviewee. The transcripts of each interview were then content analysed to draw out the commonly shared stakeholder judgements about the impact of each intervention. A summary of the perceived penetration and impact of each intervention is presented below.

5.1 CAPACITY PLANNER AND ORIGINAL EQUIPMENT SERVICE PLANNER

There was a consensus amongst interviewees that this intervention had helped in the planning of the workload on site. However, it was felt that there was a need for the planners to consult more with the shopfloor staff. It was also felt that there were limits to how much the work on site could be planned due to external factors.

> *"The appointment of a Capacity Planner and OES Planner certainly gave a clearer indication of the work required, and effectively plan the work behind Packaging.... I still believe there are certain levels of improvement that can be done to these two roles interacting more with shopfloor supervisors to help them plan"*

> *"On site, probably yes, it has helped...I'm not so sure it's helped that much in terms of influencing factors outside this site because we still get panics, we still get panics, we still get people at other sites not following systems and procedures causing problems"*

5.2 INTRODUCTION OF APPRAISALS

It was reported in the interviews that only a limited number of staff had received appraisals. Furthermore, it was felt that the quality of the appraisals which had been undertaken may have been poor, and staff may not have found them very beneficial.

> *"I don't think we've gone down deep enough. Certainly the management team have done theirs and each manager has done a number of his people...Not sure staff have found them beneficial...whilst we've got the system in place, I don't necessarily think we've got the right follow-up"*

5.3 RELOCATION OF HAND-PACK

There was a perception amongst the majority of those interviewed that this intervention had been successful in improving the environmental conditions of those employees within Hand-pack. The main benefit was the move away from the noise of the cranes in the storage areas.

"This has helped reduce the noise from the cranes...there's more natural light, as well as a bit more space "

5.4 INTERVENTIONS TO IMPROVE HOUSEKEEPING

Most of the interviewees felt that the interventions to improve housekeeping on site had been successful. In particular, they reported that the 'Dream Team' and the restructuring of the Housekeeping Review had certainly improved cleanliness on site. It would also appear that the interventions had been effective in terms of encouraging staff to take more pride in their own particular work areas.

"The insurance company were very impressed on housekeeping"

"They [the staff] certainly take it upon themselves now to clean rather than saying "It's not my job, it's Mary's".... We hold regular Housekeeping audits which is actually done by one of the safety reps....they're going to be perhaps a bit more critical...rather than covering for each other as they might have done in the past"

5.5 TEAM BRIEFINGS AND QUARTERLY COMMUNICATIONS

There was a perception amongst those managers who were interviewed that the daily team briefings had been effective in improving communication. However, the quarterly communication with senior management appeared to have been less successful.

"The daily ones give people the ideal vehicle to say what they think"

"The quarterly ones have fell into a bit of a disrepute. There hasn't been a formal quarterly [meeting] for three quarters of a year now. It's something that he [the site manager] is intending to resurrect"

"We went into very detailed communication sessions with the management team to get the site ready for the implementation of BPCS [change in packaging operation].... that went particularly well"

"There is a definite communication vacuum on site which I [the site manager] intend to correct"

5.6 FRAMED DISPLAY POSTERS AND HANDOUTS OF COMPANY OBJECTIVES

The success of this intervention in clarifying the company's goals, had been limited by the uncertainty created as a result of the merger with another organisation.

"That is probably one area where the risk factor has probably escalated because of the uncertainty with what's happening in the Group.... the movement of Domicile, the uncertainty of the pension scheme"

"Initially when the merger thing first came on board there was (sic) literally a lot of new faces, ideas, different standards.... and the idea was set up, the Vision as they call it, and that was well documented.... Unfortunately over the period of the merger.... They've had a rough deal in terms of the City and the papers and that's started people wondering and fearing 'Who are these people?'"

5.7 JOB ENLARGEMENT IN MACHINE PACK

Job design within Machine-pack was changed dramatically. At the time of the original risk assessment, employees in this area worked directly from customer 'stock orders' (details of what customers had ordered). Under this system, the appropriate quantities of the goods to be packed were delivered from stock to the packing machine with packing instructions. However, in order to improve the efficiency of product storage and supply, the job was re-designed. Instead of just packing at the machines, staff were also required to gather the appropriate quantities of goods from stock, and to then get the goods ready to be packed on the machines. To achieve this, the 'stock order' system in Machine-pack was abolished and replaced by job cards. The job cards detailed what needed to be taken from stock and indicated how orders should be packed. As staff finished each job, they were given another card. Under the new system the section became self-sufficient in the supply of products from stock, and in the way goods were prepared for packing. It was reported that this change was successful in making the job more interesting and reduced the pressure that employees were under. However, it was noted that problems still arose when there were delays in the delivery of products to the site.

"It [customers' orders] was creating quite an excessive amount of pressure.... You might get a very large order from a customer requiring large amounts of packaging time and you've got your deadline to achieve a customer order. With it going back to the packaging shop...actually should reduce the stress"

"There are still pressures but I don't believe the pressures are anywhere as great as they were. That's because, I believe, we are a lot smarter in how we progress material through the Packaging shop...you can see clear evidence of that with the way the availability has gone up.... We're hitting record levels of availability...what it doesn't do is take pressure off late deliveries...if that's coming in late and it's been promised early, you've got to push it through"

5.8 TRAINING SCHEDULE AND CONTINUOUS IMPROVEMENT

The managers reported that whilst the new training schedule had been successful in improving the quality of training on site, there were still areas where more training was required.

"The [training events] have done some very positive things, where they've certainly made people open their eyes and see what can be changed"

"The [training] got unfairly a bad name. Rather than looking at it as a methodology for continuous improvement, I think the shopfloor saw it as a methodology for reducing work and cutting jobs. So it got a bad press...Although the people who did participate...were reasonably enthusiastic...it was the pressure that they were under when they were back on the shopfloor, to say to the people 'Well we've got to change this'"

5.9 IDENTIFICATION OF 'AT RISK' AREAS THROUGH RISK ASSESSMENT

The managers reported that a lot of work had gone into carrying out thorough risk assessments of all activities and areas of the site. There were also new systems in place to ensure that the required actions were taken to address more 'tangible' physical hazards and risks.

> *"We've done a heck of a lot of work on that. We set ourselves a target by the end of August to have all areas in the warehouse and packaging operation, all activities, risk assessed and we've done that...all it is now is...to make sure we carry out all the actions we've laid out"*

Commentary on the Evaluation Process

The interventions reported in this case study were generally a product of the fundamental changes that were occurring in the organisation, and as a result, at the packaging site itself. From the stakeholder interviews, evidence emerged that many of these appeared to be well received. The fact that common threads and comments emerged from interviews with a variety of stakeholders, added weight to the conclusions drawn about the impact of the various changes. Although it would have proved informative to carry out a more quantitative evaluation, the widespread agreement on the impact of the interventions confirmed the usefulness of stakeholder interviews as an evaluation tool.

6. LEARNING POINTS

6.1 INTERVIEWING OF STAFF

During much of this project staff were anxious over their future and that of the company. In order to ensure that they felt relaxed and able to express their honest opinions, they were interviewed on a one-to-one basis in a room away from their immediate work area. They were be assured that the interview was completely confidential, and that they might terminate it at any time. They were also offered tea and coffee during their interview. A relaxed atmosphere was achieved and this facilitated the collection of an extensive amount of detailed information especially during the different types of interviews.

6.2 SELECTION OF STEERING GROUP MEMBERS

Ideally, the Steering Group members should include senior and middle management, and representatives from Occupational Health, Health and Safety, Personnel, trade unions as well as the employees involved in the project. In this case study, management expressed their wish for selection of Steering Group members to be a democratic process. However, at the same time, they also insisted that they would like some input into the selection. Management felt that employee representatives should be able to co-operate with managers and feel able to express their opinions.

6.3 PROJECT TITLE

A suitable title should be chosen for the project which will help to 'sell' it to both staff and management. It had to be non-threatening, but meaningful. In this case study, several managers expressed a view that the word 'stress' should not be included in the title. They felt that it focused on the negative side of work and health rather than on the positive. It was agreed by all Steering Group members that the project should be titled 'The Occupational Health Programme'.

6.4 EXPERT EVALUATIONS

For a number of reasons it was not possible to carry out a quantitative evaluation of the impact of the interventions in this case study. However, interviews with managers and stakeholders provided a rich source of information about the perceived effectiveness of each intervention. The use of interviews with stakeholders provides one way of evaluating interventions often with minimal disruption. This strategy is particularly useful in times of organisational instability or widespread uncertainty. Ideally, these data are then validated against other relevant information.

6.5 MAKING THE MOST OF CHANGE AND TURBULENCE

There was a great deal of turbulence and change within this organisation throughout the project. Implementing organisational interventions during such times is a challenging process. Strategic and business goals tend to become paramount to the organisation during periods of rapid change. This can make it difficult to work towards a coherent package of interventions that addresses problems of employee health. However, the risk assessment, in fact, provided a large amount of information that could be used by the organisation.

The company were able to draw upon the results of the risk assessment when implementing the new management's programme of change. Change driven from other concerns of the organisation were shaped into interventions that tackled some of the problems identified by the risk assessment. The intervention which changed the way the job was done in Machine-pack was an example of how such an approach was used to good effect. Open dialogue between those carrying out the risk assessment and those designing and implementing change was essential in order to make such a strategy work.

PART III

APPENDICES

APPENDIX I
CALCULATION AND INTERPRETATION OF ODDS RATIOS

The Odds Ratio (OR) statistic indicates the likelihood of having a particular negative health outcome in the 'inadequate reporting' group relative to those who are not reporting the work characteristic as 'inadequate', in a case-control study. That is, the ratio of the incidence of a negative outcome in the group exposed to an inadequate work characteristic divided by the corresponding incidence in the group not exposed to that inadequate work characteristic. Details of calculating and interpreting the OR, establishing statistical significance, recoding the data, and performing the computer-based analysis are described below.

1.1 CALCULATING AN ODDS RATIO

Having presented the data in 2x2 contingency table (as in Figure 1 below), the formula for calculating the Odds Ratio is:

$$OR = \frac{a/c}{b/d} = \frac{ad}{bc}$$

a = frequency of reporting inadequate work characteristic and negative outcome
b = frequency of reporting inadequate work characteristic but not negative outcome
c = frequency of not reporting inadequate work characteristic and but reporting negative outcome
d = frequency of not reporting inadequate work characteristic and not reporting negative outcome

		DISEASE		
		Yes	No	
EXPOSURE	Yes	a	b	a + b
	No	c	d	c + d
		a + c	b + d	a + b + c + d

**Figure 1: Presentation of data from a case control study
in a 2x2 contingency table**

1.2 INTERPRETING AN ODDS RATIO

The null value OR is 1. That is, if there is no relationship between inadequate work characteristic and a negative outcome, OR = 1, and those reporting the work characteristic as inadequate are just as likely to have the negative outcome as those not reporting 'inadequate'. An OR > 1 represents a positive association between inadequate work characteristic and negative outcome, with the value of the OR indicating the number of times more likely the 'inadequate' group is to have the negative outcome than the 'not inadequate' group is. For example, if OR = 3.9, those reporting the work characteristic as inadequate are 3.9 times as likely to have the negative outcome as those not reporting it as inadequate.

1.3 STATISTICAL SIGNIFICANCE OF AN ODDS RATIO ASSOCIATION

Although an OR >1 indicates a positive association between inadequate work characteristic and negative outcome, it does not necessarily follow that this statistical relationship is significant at the established level (p < 0.05). There are two sets of values through which the statistical significance of an OR can be assured: the p value of a chi-square statistic and the confidence interval of the OR itself.

1.4 CHI-SQUARE TEST STATISTIC

For discrete data, in the form of a 2x2 contingency table, the simplest and most common method to determine the statistical significance of differences between exposure and negative outcomes is the use of the chi-square test. The p value associated with a chi-square statistic is the indicator of significance. Any value of p less than or equal to 0.05 (p < 0.05) indicates that there is, at most, only a 5% probability of observing an association as large or larger than that found in the study by chance alone, given that there is really no association between exposure and the negative outcome (i.e. there is a 95% probability that the association is true and did not occur by chance alone). The likelihood ratio chi-square statistic is currently used as the most appropriate statistic indicating significance for the OR (Howell, 1992, p.144; Hosmer and Lemeshow, 1989).

The p value arrived at is a function of the magnitude of the difference between the two groups or the strength of their association, and the size of the sample. For this reason, the p value should be considered as a guide to action rather than a 'hard and fast' rule on which to base a conclusion about the role of a risk factor. To overcome this difficulty, a related but far more informative measure to evaluate the role of chance, the confidence interval (CI), can be reported (Hennekens and Buring, 1987, p. 252).

1.5 CONFIDENCE INTERVALS

The confidence interval for an OR represents the range within which the true magnitude of the effect lies within a certain degree of certainty. For example, an OR of 3.9 with 95% CI of 1.3 to 5.2, indicates that the best estimate of the increased risk is 3.9; however, we can be 95% confident that the true risk is no less than 1.3 and no greater than 5.2.

The CI can provide all the information of the p value in terms of whether the association is statistically significant at the specified 0.05 level. If the null value (i.e. 1) is included in the 95% confidence interval, then the corresponding p value is, by definition, greater than 0.05, and therefore not statistically significant. However, if the null value (1) is *not* included in the interval, then the corresponding p value is less than 0.05 and the association *is* statistically significant (Hennekens and Buring, 1987, p. 253).

The confidence intervals can be calculated using the following formula:

$$CI = (ad/bc) \exp [\pm Z \sqrt{(1/a + 1/b + 1/c + 1/d)}]$$
$$(\text{for 95\% confidence i.e. } p \leq 0.05, Z=1.96)$$

For example,

$$CI = (5) \exp [\pm 1.96 \sqrt{(1/3 + 1/6 + 1/2 + 1/20)}]$$
$$= (5) \exp (\pm 2.008)$$

$$\text{lower} = 5\,e^{-2.008}$$
$$= 0.67$$

$$\text{upper} = 5\,e^{+2.008}$$
$$= 37.34$$

In this example the OR of 5 is not significant at a 95% confidence level because the null value (1) falls between the lower and upper confidence limits (0.67 and 37.34).

The exact p value and the confidence interval together provide the most information about the role of chance in the OR calculation (Hennekens and Buring, 1987, p. 253).

1.6 RECODING DATA FOR ODDS RATIOS

To carry out analyses using ORs, all data must be recoded into dichotomised variables.

The work characteristics variables are measured on a 0 to 5 scale, where 0 is not applicable, 1 is inadequate, 2 is slightly inadequate, 3 is neither, 4 is good, and 5 is excellent. These variables should be recoded in the first instance as follows: 1 and 2 as 1 (response), 4 and 5 as 0 (reference), and 3 and 0 as 'missing'.

However, if the data are skewed in either direction, or if the sample size is small through removing data through the recoding process, this may mean that ORs can not be calculated as a zero cell is present, e.g.:

$$\frac{0/15}{3/23} = e$$

There are a number of ways to overcome this problem. First, 0.5 can be added to the count in each cell and the Odds Ratio recalculated (see Hosmer and Lemeshow, 1989; Goodman, 1971). Alternatively, there are two other procedures for recoding which can be used:

i.   recode 3 (the neither response) as 0 (reference) rather than 'missing', or

ii.   recode the data on the basis of a mean split for each item, i.e. find the mean response (1-5) for each item and recode those reporting the item as more inadequate than the mean response as 1 (response), and those reporting the item as better than the mean as 0.

The outcome variables should be recoded on the basis of either:

i.   suggested extreme or 'risk' levels of the outcome in question, e.g. for 'worn out' scores, recode those with a score > 25 as 1, and those with < 25 as 0, or use the score 1 standard deviation above the mean as a cut-off; and for 'risk' drinking levels, recode those drinking > 22 units per week as 1, and those drinking < 22 as 0, or

ii.   the mean scores of the assessment sample, e.g. for 'worn out' or 'tense' scores, recode those with a score > the mean score as 1, and those with < the mean as 0.

1.7 PERFORMING ODDS RATIOS ANALYSIS

The analysis of the risk assessment data is carried out according to the logic and procedures described above using the statistical package SPSS 6.1 for the Power Macintosh. Within this package, the procedures for performing this analysis are within the 'Crosstabs' section of the 'Summarize' procedures in the 'Statistics' menu.

In 'Crosstabs', select the variables to be examined as potential risk factors (i.e. work characteristics and conditions variables) and insert them into the 'rows' box. Then select the outcome variable to be tested for association with the work characteristics and insert it into the 'columns' box. In the 'Statistics' option, select the 'risk' box and the 'Chi-Square' box.

In the output, the OR for each pair of variables is the 'case-control Relative Risk' value. If the lower 95% confidence bound corresponding to this value is >1 then the OR is significant, but for the exact p value, use the Likelihood Ratio values from the Chi-square tests.

Finally, it is useful to check one or two of the OR values and CI values by calculating them by hand to ensure the procedures and codings have been carried out correctly.

APPENDIX II
GLOSSARY

Audit of existing management control and employee support systems (Management Systems Audit): This is an audit exercise designed to assess the nature, availability and adequacy of the measures already taken by the organisation to control work stress and manage employee health and welfare. Information for the audit is gathered through interviews with key stakeholders, and by examining organisational documentation (e.g. policies) and reports (e.g. absence levels, figures on the uptake of Occupational Health services).

Causal inference: This is the drawing of conclusions about cause and effect. To be able to say, on the basis of evidence, that A causes B is to make a causal inference.

Common method variance: This is a phenomenon that may occur when several sets of data are collected using the same method (e.g. through a questionnaire survey). It is possible that any relationship between those data sets may largely reflect the fact that they were collected in the same way.

Conceptual validity: This relates to the overall consistency of ideas, their internal logic.

Concurrent validity: This is the extent to which one set of data is related to, or predicts, another set of data collected at the same time.

Consensus agreement: This is the degree to which members of a group agree in their judgements about something, e.g. the majority of employees reporting that an aspect of their work is inadequate. In the current project, when identifying major stressors, for a group which reported a large number of problems, a *cut-off* of 70 % agreement (consensus) was taken. Where fewer and less serious problems were identified, this level was adjusted downwards to around 50 %.

Control strategies: Interventions designed to reduce the exposure to a health and safety (stress) problem, or to minimise the harm that may be caused by the problem through personal protection or treatment.

Focus group: A managed group discussion designed to elicit information about a particular topic.

General Well-Being Questionnaire: A health questionnaire designed at Nottingham by Tom Cox and his colleagues that is based on an assessment of non-specific symptoms of general malaise. It contains measures of feeling 'worn out' (tired, emotional, confused etc.) and 'tense' (nervous, anxious, jittery, etc.).

Halo effect: This occurs when judgements, or reports, on particular aspects of a situation are unduly influenced by an overarching opinion, attitude or judgement. A halo effect 'contaminates' the data and reduces their usefulness.

Headline data: In the current project, 'headline' data are those for the total occupational group, not broken down by any sub-divisions of the group or by responses to particular questions. Because of the complexity of most of the situations in the case studies, the headline data covering an intervention usually only set the scene for more specific enquiries (e.g. looking at the data with reference to the degree of involvement in that intervention).

Health profile: In the current project, this is presentation and interpretation (or profiling) of data from the various health measures used in the risk assessment.

Health related behaviour(s): These are behaviours that are related in some way, and possibly help determine, health status. For example, smoking and drinking, the quality of sleep, involvement in exercise, etc.

Job satisfaction: This is a measure of how happy, or satisfied, employees are with their job.

Likely risk factor: In the present project, a likely risk factor is defined as an aspect of the design and management of work for which there is evidence of an association with health.

Management control and employee support systems: These are the organisational systems and initiatives already in place to try to reduce or otherwise control the problem of work stress, and to support employees who experience such stress.

Mental and physiological function: Mental function relates to cognitive activities such as perceiving, thinking, remembering and believing. Physiological functioning relates to the body's more physical and chemical processes and is often used to talk about the way organ and related systems work.

Meta-analysis: A method used to draw out the common findings from a number of different studies. This involves combining the data from those studies and subjecting them to a particular form of statistical analysis.

Musculoskeletal discomfort and pain: This refers to pain and discomfort in the bones and joints, and in the muscles and other soft tissue that relate to the person's skeleton and to their movements.

Normative group: A population-based comparison group used, in the present project, to give meaning to the health scores.

On-going change: In the present project, on-going change is used to refer to change that is already underway at the time of the risk assessment (or when the subsequent interventions and evaluations were carried out).

Organisational documentation and data: This is information held by the organisation that can be utilised in a risk assessment, in the audit of existing management control and employee support systems, or in the evaluation of any interventions.

Organisational health: This refers to the healthiness of the organisation and is separate from that of the individual employee. It is close to the concept of organisational culture, but goes beyond this to incorporate aspects of organisational structure and function.

Organisational learning: The processes by which organisations learn, and the content of what they learnt.

Organisationally acceptable scripts: In this project, organisationally acceptable scripts are the structured accounts (or stories) that Steering Groups develop to describe the risk assessment findings in a way which is not threatening, and which facilitates further actions.

Pathology: This is a state of ill-health or disorder. In the present project, it is used to refer to some underlying and long standing problem in the organisation that drives, or otherwise links several of the likely risk factors.

Primary prevention: This refers to tackling a problem at source rather than the symptoms of the problem. In the current project, this focuses on changes to the design and management of work.

Psychometric (measures): These are technical measures of a psychological nature, that give some indication of a person's thought processes. Psychometric measures have a number of properties including reliability (see glossary), validity (that they measure what they purport to measure) and fairness.

Psychosocial and organisational hazards: These refer to problems in the design and management of work, or social and organisational contexts, that have the potential for harming the health of individual employees or that of their organisation.

Reliability: This refers to the extent of the consistency of a measure. All measures contain some degree of error. The smaller the error contained within the measure, the more reliable the measure is.

Risk assessment: This is a procedure used to identify likely sources (causes) of harm and to make some judgement on their importance and impact based on evidence.

Risk reduction (for work stress): This is an intervention, or other action, that is designed to reduce the experience of work stress or its effects. In the current project, risk reduction is focused on the organisation, on the design and management of work, and on primary prevention.

Semi-structured (interview): This is an interview that is structured around a series of set guiding questions, but that is conducted in a flexible way that allows some freedom to interviewees in their responses and to interviewers in structuring the on-going dialogue.

Social desirability: This is a phenomenon that may affect self-report data. There may be a tendency for people to respond to questions in a way that they think is socially acceptable or valued.

Steering Group: In the current project, the Steering Group is a team of key stakeholders in the risk management process that works together with the project team to guide, market and support, and validate the overall process.

Stressor: This is an aspect of work that has the potential for harm to the health of the individual employee through the experience of stress.

Structured sample (of interviewees): This is a sample of staff that is representative of the larger group to which they belong and which reflects the structure of that group. Members of the sample are chosen at random from the larger group but in a way that reflects its structure.

Triangulation: This is a strategy used for checking the reliability of a set of data by comparing it with at least two other sets of data collected by different means.

Variable: This is a particular type or unit of data or set of data. A variable usually has a numerical value obtained from a measure. For example, job satisfaction and well-being are both variables.

Work Analysis Interview: In the current project, this refers to an exploratory interview that investigates the nature of the person's job, the problems that the person and their colleagues face with their work, the related sources of satisfaction, and how such factors might be expressed in terms of the health of the individual or of the overall organisation.

Working conditions: In the current project, these refer to the sum of the (person's) work, work systems, work equipment and management environment, as well as their social and organisational contexts.

Work Environment Survey: In the present project, this refers to an assessment instrument that measures exposure to, and the adequacy of, those characteristics of work design and management that have been identified as potential risk factors. The Work Environment Survey is tailored to the needs and context of particular occupational groups (the assessment groups).